C000006619

# qabalah
 *a beginner's guide*

# qaBaLaɧ

 *a beginner's guide*

KATE RHEEDERS

## Hodder & Stoughton

A MEMBER OF THE HODDER HEADLINE GROUP

Illustrations by Mirella Brummer.

Order queries: please contact Bookpoint Ltd, 39 Milton Park, Abingdon, Oxon OX14 4TD. Telephone: (44) 01235 400414, Fax: (44) 01235 400454. Lines are open from 9.00–6.00, Monday to Saturday, with a 24-hour message answering service. Email address: orders@bookpoint.co.uk

*British Library Cataloguing in Publication Data*
A catalogue record for this title is available from The British Library

ISBN 0 340 74262 3

First published 1996
This edition published 1999
Impression number  10 9 8 7 6 5 4 3 2 1
Year                        2005 2004 2003 2002 2001 2000 1999

Typeset by Transet Limited, Coventry, England.
Printed in Great Britain for Hodder & Stoughton Educational, a division of Hodder Headline plc, 338 Euston Road, London NW1 3BH by Cox and Wyman Limited, Reading, Berks.

### *Dedication*

This book was channelled through by my Guide, Shaul, who lived in the Ukraine during the nineteenth century. It is dedicated to my son, Ockert Rheeders.

Special thanks to Chris Stormer for her encouragement.

Thank you to Jackie Casarin, Liz Harris and Chris Stormer for their proof-reading and constructive criticism.

# CONTENTS

# INTRODUCTION

*Blessed is the man who finds wisdom, the man who gains
understanding, for she is more profitable than silver and
yields better return than gold. She is more precious than
rubies; nothing you desire can compare with her. Long life
is in her right hand; in her left hand riches and honour.
Her ways are pleasant ways, and all her paths are peace.
She is a tree of life to those who embrace her, those who
lay hold of her will be blessed.*

Proverbs 3: 13–18

*T*he Qabalah is an ancient Jewish system of spiritual knowledge
*that forms the basis of the Western Tradition. All traditions, cultures
and beliefs, like rivers, start from a spring or fountain taking on
characteristics that change through time and the layout of the land
through which they flow. The Western Tradition sprang from the
Qabalah.*

*The word* Qabalah *is spelt in many different ways:* Qabalah *is
generally used in the Western Tradition,* Kabbalah *in the Jewish, and*
Cabala *in the Christian Tradition, but all refer to the same system.*

*Whichever way the name is spelt,* Qabalah *means 'to receive' and 'to
reveal'. It is important to be ready to receive the knowledge before it is
revealed to us. The Age of Aquarius is in our lives and opening up
individual awarenesses to allow the knowledge of the Qabalah to enter.*

# Where does the Qabalah come from?

There are two stories – one mystical and another factual. They are probably both correct and merely form two chapters in the same tale. The mystical story covers the conception and growth of the Qabalah and the factual one reveals its more recent history since the birth of Christ. To follow is a shortened version of these tales.

The mystical story starts with a wonderful, loving, light-filled female energy that wanted to share all of Her love. In order to do so, She created a male counterpart to assist Her in Her task. This important fact will be discussed in greater detail at a later stage. I will refer to this Mother–Father Deity as 'MF' from here onwards. MF first taught all the angels the secrets of the Qabalah. Only then was humankind, the world and all that inhabits it created.

The creative process is often compared with a mountain and a stone, with MF being the mountain and man being the stone. Although the stone comes from the mountain, it is by no means the mountain itself. To remove the stone from the mountain, a cutting device such as a chisel is required. The moment the chisel comes between the mountain and the stone, the stone ceases to be part of the mountain.

After the fall from grace, the angels gathered together and decided to share the secrets of the Qabalah with the humans so that they could create their own Paradise. Unfortunately, few listened and even fewer applied this knowledge in their lives and it was not long before the secret died with the last enlightened human being.

One of the secrets taught to the angels was the Holy Name of God. There are 72 names which refer to God in the Bible, but only one held all the secrets of the entire Qabalah. This Holy Name is Jehovah (IHVH) and consists of only four Hebrew letters. This name of God is better known as the Tetragrammaton. Its correspondences are shown on page 3.

For more information on Hebrew, please refer to Chapter 6.

| I | י | Yud | Fire | Father | Creative |
| H | ה | He | Water | Mother | Receptive |
| V | ו | Vav | Air | Son | Formative |
| H | ה | He | Earth | Daughter | Material |

This gives rise to two ideas:

- Perfect balance between the Mature Male, Young Male, Mature Female and Young Female energies create the 'perfect' human and the 'ideal' family unit.
- All living beings in the environment contain various proportions of the four elements, i.e. fire, water, air and earth.

This particular secret was very valuable to Abraham when he was given the Qabalah by God. This is dealt with in more depth in Chapter 6. Abraham passed the knowledge on to Isaac and Jacob, who in turn revealed it to Joseph. Unfortunately Joseph died before he could impart the knowledge, and, again, the chain was broken.

God, however, decided that the knowledge would be revealed to those who reached a certain level of spiritual development. Moses was such a person and his history is told in the book of Exodus.

Moses was born to Jewish parents whilst the Israelites were enslaved in Egypt. In order to save his life, his mother put him into the River Nile, where he was later found by Pharaoh's daughter. She raised him as her own son and this was possibly one of the reasons why Moses developed into the unique individual that he was. He had the benefit of both cultures, and yet he must have felt torn by conflicting feelings.

Moses led the Israelites out of Egypt, and during their journey through the desert he received the Ten Commandments from God on Mount Sinai. Moses spent a total of 40 days and 40 nights with God on two separate occasions during which time he received not only the Ten Commandments, but also the Verbal Qabalah. Moses also wrote his understanding of God's words down and these appear

as the first four books of the Old Testament.

Later, after the time of Moses, a group of enlightened men came together and started a mystical school where they taught and learned more about the practical side of the Qabalah. This school was held in secret and only a few had access to the teachings, hence the strict rules that apply today. These will be referred to later.

# Who wrote it and when?

The factual story follows the mystical story, although it is obvious that many more factors were involved in the Qabalah.

Qabalistic teachings stem mainly from three different books. The first is called the *Sepher Yetzirah*, better known as the Book of Formation. Some believe that Abraham recorded some secrets before passing on the knowledge and that the *Sepher Yetzirah* is nothing other that his writings, discovered and rewritten. These were possibly written by a man called Rabbi Akiba before the sixth century AD.

Rabbi Akiba (a Jewish mystic) apparently did not have the insight to write a book of such magnitude, which is probably where some doubt creeps in. It is not a very long book (less than 2,000 words) and it contains valuable knowledge that links the use of Gematria (the deeper meaning of Hebrew words) to the understanding of the entire universe. Gematria is discussed in Chapter 6.

The second book is called the *Zohar,* commonly referred to as the Book of Splendour. Some believe that a student of Rabbi Akiba wrote the *Zohar* and others believe it was written during the Spanish Inquisition by a man called B. Rambam.

The Spanish Inquisition was a fearful time for the enlightened elders. Not only did they fear for their lives, they also feared that the knowledge of the Qabalah would once again be lost. This is probably why the *Zohar* was written. It describes the universe as an interconnected mass of particles governed by a higher force.

Both the *Sepher Yetzirah* and the *Zohar* stress the importance of the

feminine and the masculine sides of God. This may be the relationship between the sexual and the spiritual side of people as well as the loving and assertive sides confirming that males and females were created in the image of God.

The third book, the *Sepher Bahir*, is the Book of Brilliance. Written during the thirteenth century in Spain it was believed to be one of the most important Qabalistic teachings, since it describes the universe as a multi-layered reality in which all parts are connected, and where each and every part is governed by a higher law. This was possibly written by someone who recognised the magical connection between the *Sepher Yetzirah* and the *Zohar*.

# Why is it important?

Whether we speak of the 'Age of Aquarius' or the 'New Age', it is clear that a new awareness is emerging. The previous age was one in which groups were led by enlightened individuals, gurus. The age now dawning is associated with brotherhood, co-operation and mutual encouragement. Now is the time to learn and understand one another, to heal the planet and start taking responsibility for personal happiness.

The Qabalah can assist everyone with the following:

- The expression of true feelings and thoughts to enhance relationships with others.
- The realisation that bizarre behaviour in others is not necessarily bad.
- The discovery that a balance between feminine and masculine creates harmony and peace.
- Equilibrium between outer experiences and the subsequent inner feelings.
- The realisation that apparently complex problems often have simple solutions.
- The use of resources which are widely available yet difficult to access.
- The knowledge that each individual has a unique purpose to fulfil

in the universe during this lifetime.
- The attainment and maintenance of physical, emotional and spiritual well-being.

Many more points are worthy of mention. See if you can think of any more that are of particular interest and write them down as they come to mind. You will find this a useful exercise.

# Who reads the Qabalah?

Until very recently the Qabalah was reserved for married Jewish men over the age of 40. During the Middle Ages this rule was maintained for the following reasons:

- The Jews were God's chosen people and therefore believed that the Qabalah was their property.
- During this period, education was restricted to boys and therefore very few women could read and write, let alone understand the Qabalah.
- It was believed that studying the Qabalah required maturity.
- Married men were considered more responsible.

In fact, during the Middle Ages the Qabalah was revealed only to certain Rabbis over 40; it was, and still is, one of their duties to marry and have a family.

Once the individual's awareness is acute enough to understand and accept the knowledge contained in the Qabalah, it will reveal itself.

# ḅow can we work with it?

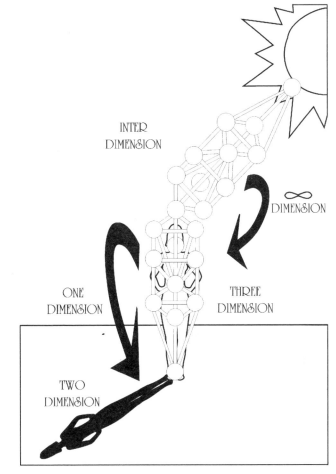

INTER
DIMENSION

∞
DIMENSION

ONE
DIMENSION

THREE
DIMENSION

TWO
DIMENSION

Diagram 1.1: Your shadow, your body and your higher self

To find out how to work with the Qabalah, study Diagram 1.1 and follow the example carefully:

7

1. When a person stands in the sun, a shadow is cast. It has length and width but no depth and is therefore two-dimensional. In order for the shadow to lift its arm, the physical body has to lift its arm. One may have a conversation with one's shadow, but it can never reply.

2. The body has length, width and depth and is therefore a three-dimensional being. This extra dimension that the body possesses gives it the ability to understand the two-dimensional shadow. It can then make the necessary movements that will allow the shadow to move.

3. Above, around, next to or within the body is an even higher, inter-dimensional being. This being understands the needs of the individual on a much higher/deeper level.

4. In order to undergo spiritual growth, an individual may need to 'lift his/her arms'. This higher being may then in turn 'lift its arms' and bring about certain situations that are nothing more than simply 'lifting the arms'.

When we understand this concept, we can recognise obstacles as growth opportunities. Instead of being victims, we can take responsibility for our lives and thereby grow on a spiritual level.

## EXERCISE 1
## The qabalistic cross exercise

This exercise is particularly effective in re-establishing contact with the inner Tree of Life and bringing with it the realisation that there is a higher, purer side to the self. By strengthening the aura it provides protection from any unwanted energies that intrude into your space. It heals the self and the planet whilst balancing the mind and body. It will clear the area and should therefore be practised prior to any Qabalistic work.

Allow enough time and space to do this exercise. It will last approximately five minutes and you will need to stretch your arms as far to the side as possible. Diagram 1.2 will clarify this exercise.

1. Stand upright with your arms next to your body without creating a stiff posture.

2. Allow your breathing to develop into a pattern where you fill your lungs to their fullest capacity, holding the breath for a few seconds and then letting it all go. Repeat this for a while and feel how the pattern starts to flow.

3. Become aware of the fact that you are doing this exercise with purpose and free from any pressure. You choose to be here, now, in this space, doing this exercise. Allow your mind to empty itself of all feelings and thoughts.

4. Touch your forehead between the eyebrows with the forefinger of your right hand, hold it in that position for a short while and become aware of the higher self residing within you.

5. Now say out loud:    ATEH
   Pronounced:    A-T-E-H
   Meaning:    'For Thine'

6. Move the forefinger of your right hand from your forehead, in a straight line down to your genital area and while holding it there for a short while, become aware of your whole body.

7. Now say out loud:    MALCHUTH
   Pronounced:    M-A-L-CH-U-T
   Meaning:    'Kingdom'

8. Move the forefinger of your right hand to your right shoulder and while holding it in that position for a short while, become aware of your will-power.

9. Now say out loud:    VE GEBURAH
   Pronounced:    V-E G-E-B-OO-R-A-H
   Meaning:    'The Power'

10. Move the forefinger of your right hand from your right shoulder, in a straight line across your chest, to your left shoulder and while holding your finger there for a short while, become aware of all your love energy.

11. Now say out loud:    VE GEDULAH
    Pronounced:    V-E G-E-D-OO-L-A-H
    Meaning:    'The Glory'

12. Clasp your two hands together in a praying fashion over your heart and become aware of the space around you. Realise that within you are all the powers of love and will.

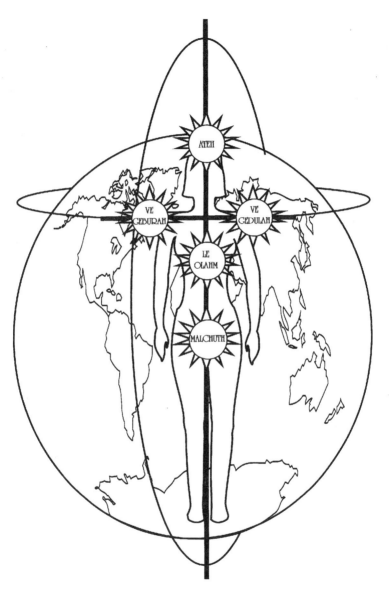

Diagram 1.2: The Qabalistic cross exercise

13. Now say out loud:     LE OLAHM
    Pronounced:     L-E O-L-A-M
    Meaning:         'For ever and ever'
14. Extend both your arms as if you are standing as a cross and
    visualise both the lines that you have drawn over your body
    as bright, shining light.  Realise that you have become a
    glowing cross extending all the way up, down, left and right
    embracing the whole world.
15. Now say out loud:     AMEN
16. Allow yourself to realise the meaning of this exercise and how
    it can and will assist you in your Qabalistic work.

# ThE TREE Of LifE

*Now the Lord God had planted a garden in the east, in
Eden; and there He put the man He had formed. And the
Lord God made all kinds of trees to grow out of the ground
– trees that were pleasing to the eye and good for food.
In the middle of the garden were the tree of life and the
tree of the knowledge of good and evil.*

Genesis 2: 8–9

*T*he Tree of Life is a summary of the entire Qabalah and it is often
referred to as the 'map of the universe'. It contains all levels of
experience. It includes the outer and inner worlds and the relationship
between them. It holds the key to the body, the personality, the soul
and the spirit.

Notice in the example used in Chapter 1 (Diagram 1.1) the Tree of Life
is present in the shadow, the body and also in the higher self.

## ThE BASIC mAP

Have a piece of A4 paper and a pen ready before continuing with
the basic map of the Tree.

The Tree of Life consists of 10 numbered spheres, 1 unnumbered
sphere and 22 paths that connect the numbered spheres. The
spheres are all located on three columns. The numbered spheres

follow in sequence, which will be easy to realise once the Tree has been drawn in total.

Here is a quick guide (only 16 steps) to drawing a two-dimensional version of the Tree of Life. Start by folding the piece of paper in half, and then in half again, so that when opened it is creased into quarters. Draw a circle (approximately 1 inch) in the centre where the cross is formed by the folds.

1. This sphere is numbered 6, named Tiph-Ereth and is attributed to the ego. Write that information inside the circle.
2. Draw a line on the horizontal centre fold of the paper from the left to the right without cutting through Tiph-Ereth and mark this as the Veil.
3. Draw on the vertical centre fold, below Tiph-Ereth, another two circles, with the bottom one almost touching the bottom of the page.
4. The sphere below Tiph-Ereth is named Yesod, is numbered 9 and is attributed to the subconscious and the past.
5. The bottom sphere is named Malchuth, is numbered 10 and is attributed to the external world and the five senses.
6. Draw on the vertical centre fold, above Tiph-Ereth, another two circles, with the top one almost touching the top of the page.
7. The sphere above Tiph-Ereth is named Daath, is the unnumbered sphere and is attributed to knowledge.
8. Draw a line from the left of the paper to the right, level with Daath but not cutting through it. Mark this the Abyss.
9. The sphere at the top of the page is named Kether, is numbered 1 and is attributed to the pure spirit of the self. You have just completed all the spheres on the centre column.
10. Fold the outer edges of the paper towards the centre fold and crease the paper, creating eight vertical rectangles.
11. Draw halfway between Kether and Daath, on the outer folds of the paper, two circles.
12. The sphere on the right is named Chockmah, is numbered 2 and is attributed to spiritual will and the one on the left is named Binah, is numbered 3 and is attributed to spiritual love.
13. Draw another two circles below Chockmah and Binah, this time halfway between Daath and Tiph-Ereth.

14. The one on the right is named Chesed, is numbered 4 and is attributed to individual love; the one on the left is named Geburah, is numbered 5 and is attributed to the individual will.
15. The last two circles are drawn halfway between Tiph-Ereth and Yesod, on the two outer folds.
16. The sphere on the right is named Netzach, is numbered 7 and is attributed to feeling; the one on the left is named Hod, numbered 8 and is attributed to thought.

See Diagram 2.1, The basic map of the Tree of Life.

Table 2.1 shows a brief summary of the Tree of Life that you have completed:

Table 2.1

| 1 | Kether | Centre | Pure spirit |
|---|--------|--------|-------------|
| 2 | Chockmah | Right | Spiritual will |
| 3 | Binah | Left | Spiritual love |
| D | Daath | Centre | Knowledge |
| 4 | Chesed | Right | Individual love |
| 5 | Geburah | Left | Individual will |
| 6 | Tiph-Ereth | Centre | Ego |
| 7 | Netzach | Right | Feeling |
| 8 | Hod | Left | Thought |
| 9 | Yesod | Centre | Subconscious |
| 10 | Malchuth | Centre | External world |

The Tree of Life was created from sphere 1, down to 10. By using different coloured pencils, connect the numbered spheres in sequence and notice that a flash enters the Tree at the top, moves towards the right and then to the left, until it reaches the final sphere at the bottom of the Tree. This represents a lightning flash, so often seen in nature and is referred to as the 'Lightning Flash of Creation'.

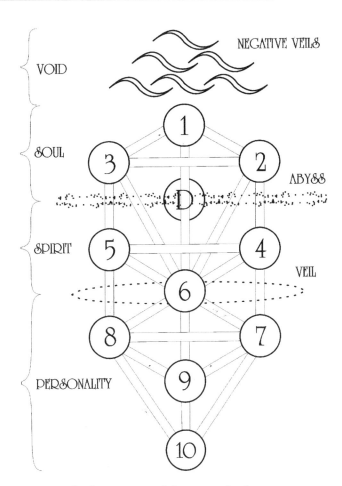

Diagram 2.1: The basic map of the Tree of Life

# The nUMBERED sphERES

Notice how the Tree is cut into three parts by the Veil and the Abyss. The Veil cuts through Tiph-Ereth separating spheres 7, 8, 9 and 10 from the rest of the Tree, while the Abyss cuts through Daath

separating spheres 1, 2 and 3 from the middle section, which consists of spheres 4, 5 and 6.

Within every person are masculine and feminine qualities that are associated with the right and left sides respectively, i.e. the right is masculine and the left is feminine. The right-hand side of the Tree contains the masculine characteristics and the left the feminine ones.

The Tree of Life also has a positive and a negative side. This rule can be compared with the moon, which when full merely reflects the light of the sun. The moon is never fully visible to the eye, always hiding its dark side. The same principle is active in the Tree of Life. There is a dark (negative) and a light (positive) side to almost all the spheres. This is not the same as the masculine and feminine sides, although they are also referred to as the positive/light and negative/ dark sides.

This concept is studied in Chapter 3 using the three-dimensional Tree of Life (Diagram 3.3).

## The personality

The personality consists of spheres 7, 8, 9 and 10 and can be broken down as follows:

| Malchuth | 10 | Malchuth means 'Kingdom' and is associated with the external world and senses, i.e. seeing hearing, feeling, smelling and tasting. |
| Yesod | 9 | Yesod means 'Foundation' and is associated with the subconscious, lower unconscious and all knowledge from the past. |
| Hod | 8 | Hod means 'Glory' and is associated with thinking, the mind or the intellect. |
| Netzach | 7 | Netzach means 'Victory' and is associated with feeling. |

From this we can deduce the following:

- The body is the 'window' available to the soul through which life can be experienced. By increasing the sensory awareness, strong connections can be made between the spiritual (inner) and physical (outer) realms.
- The top part of Yesod contains all knowledge from the past and therefore has more effect on the thoughts and feelings. The bottom part contains all the survival skills, such as material needs and therefore has more effect on the physical bodies/worlds. Very often these two functions get muddled up and past experiences influence survival, causing an imbalance.
- When active in Hod, thoughts are at play. These may be sparked off by a feeling (Netzach), as a result of the five senses (Malchuth) or from a memory (Yesod).
- Feelings, positive and negative, are all attributed to Netzach. Feelings are sometimes triggered off by thoughts (Hod), by a past experience (Yesod) or sometimes by hearing a song (Malchuth). Feelings and emotions are not the same. Feelings come from within (Netzach) and emotions come from an experience through the senses (Malchuth) that triggers past memories (Yesod).
- Everyday existence moves within these four spheres. When awake, either feelings, thoughts or sensations are active, creating movement around the outer triangle; Malchuth, Hod and Netzach. Yesod is the channel through which dreams reach the conscious mind. This level of awareness is active when nostalgia sets in.
- Malchuth, Hod and Netzach are the three spheres that represent the present or the actual. The spheres above the Veil all represent the future or the potential whilst Yesod is the past. The past is carried within the present and it is therefore important to 'dump some of the garbage' that influences the present and indirectly then affects the future.
- The smallest connection that is made on this level of the Tree will bring about evolution and growth further up the Tree. Every moment of life is therefore contributing to eventual spiritual growth.
- When the map of the Tree of Life is placed on the front of the body (Diagram 1.1), Hod is on the right and Netzach on the left. Hod is a masculine and Netzach a feminine energy.

- Spheres 7, 8 and 10 and 7, 8 and 9 form triangles pointing down towards earth. Symbolically this confirms how the individual has manifested into this world with his/her particular personality.

# Tbe soul

The soul consists of Tiph-Ereth (sphere 6), Geburah (sphere 5) and Chesed (sphere 4). In more detail, this appears as follows:

Tiph-Ereth    6    Tiph-Ereth means Beauty and Harmony and is associated with the centre, 'I' or the 'ego'.

Geburah    5    Geburah means Strength and is associated with individual will.

Chesed    4    Chesed means Mercy and is associated with individual love.

From this we can deduce the following:

- Tiph-Ereth is not only associated with the 'centre' of the being, but is also in the centre of the Tree of Life. Every sphere, except Malchuth is directly connected to Tiph-Ereth. Some believe only the evidence of the senses. In other words they only accept what they experience through Malchuth as being real, yet Malchuth is not even connected to Tiph-Ereth.
- Tiph-Ereth is the link between the spirit (spheres 3, 2 and 1) and the personality (spheres 7, 8, 9 and 10). When living from Tiph-Ereth, i.e. a centred life, spiritual awareness can be manifested, creating beauty and harmony.
- Instead of perceiving oneself as a body with a personality and a soul attached, realise it is rather a soul with a body and a personality attached. This perception will bring about a state in which one can get in touch with all feelings and love, will and thoughts, future and past, resulting in complete balance.
- Strength is a higher form of thought and Geburah (strength) lies above Hod (thought) on the right pillar of the Tree. Both these energies are masculine.

- Love is a higher form of feelings and Chesed (love) lies above Netzach (feelings) on the left pillar of the Tree. Both these are feminine energies.
- The three spheres of the soul, 4, 5 and 6, form a triangle pointing down towards the two triangles of the personality. Symbolically this brings the qualities of the soul into the realm of the personality.

## Tbe spirit

The spirit consists of Binah (sphere 3), Chockmah (sphere 2) and Kether (sphere 1). They are as follows:

| Binah | 3 | Binah means Understanding and is associated with spiritual love. |
| Chockmah | 2 | Chockmah means Wisdom and is associated with spiritual will. |
| Kether | 1 | Kether means Crown and is associated with pure spirit. |

From this we can deduce, the following:

- All three spheres lie above the Abyss and are therefore only available during very peaceful periods. These periods are generally experienced in nature when all the spheres below the Abyss are in total balance and harmony. The energies from these three spheres are channelled into the personality through Tiph-Ereth.
- The mystical story told in the Introduction of this book may be connected to these three spheres, Kether being the loving, light-filled being, Chockmah the male counterpart and Binah the creation. This ties up with the first and second worlds, which will be discussed later in this chapter.
- These three spheres form a triangle that points upwards and all spiritual needs lie within this realm. These spiritual needs are manifested in the soul in a spiral action through the Abyss, where the first triangle is duplicated in reverse. In other words what is on the right-hand side on the spiritual level is now on the left-hand side on the soul level, and what was on top is now at the bottom. This spiral action can be compared to the DNA structure.

- Similarly the right brain lies in Binah (see Chapter 3). The left-hand side of the body is controlled by this side of the brain. The same is applicable to the opposite side.
- Below Binah (spiritual love) lies Geburah (individual will) and Chockmah (spiritual will) lies above Chesed (individual love). Kether (pure spirit) is a higher form of Tiph-Ereth (ego) and they both lie on the central column.

Notice that due to a spiritual need, in order for the soul to grow, the necessary situations in this life that will create that growth is manifested into the personality. The spirit is like a radio wave, the soul like a radio and the personality like the music; the finer the tuning of the transistor radio, the clearer the music. In other words, the personality is not formed and developed by chance, but is rather directly related to the lesson on the spiritual level.

# The unnumbered sphere

The only unnumbered sphere in the Tree of Life is Daath. Daath lies within the Abyss, below Kether and above Tiph-Ereth and can be shown with position only in a two-dimensional version of the Tree.

Daath is attributed to 'Knowledge'. We encounter knowledge every moment of our lives. There will always be new information available. Yet not all knowledge is understood. Daath has no dimensions yet has all dimensions. The knowledge of Daath is without understanding, which comes from Binah. There are many people who have knowledge without understanding.

Daath lies in the Abyss and is the gate to the reverse side of the Tree of Life (Tree of Evil) which is the area from which demons and diseases come. It can therefore be said that whatever comes through the Abyss is the opposite to what lies above it. Everything below the Abyss has duality – positive and negative, dark and light; all that lies above the Abyss is without duality.

In order to understand this concept, imagine being in the spiritual world prior to reincarnating. Two soulmates have decided to

reincarnate in order to learn how to deal with love and have agreed to reincarnate and help each other with this lesson. Parents were selected and he was born a little boy called George whilst the other was born a little girl called Susan. Both grew up and met in their teens, fell in love and married during their early twenties.

George, however, is a very jealous man – not by accident but because he has to learn about love. Susan is a flirt who attracts a lot of attention from others, because this is the only way that George will learn his lesson. George and Susan have endless arguments and eventually the situation is created where George has no choice but to face his insecurities.

The knowledge of the reasons for the incarnation remains in the Abyss and although the spirit (above the Abyss) contains the understanding of this information, the soul has taken on a reversed version of the lesson of love which manifested as jealousy.

It is human nature to take life for granted so long as the going is easy. Only when we are faced with hardship and hurt do growth and understanding take place.

Imagine that George's jealousy leads Susan to take the kids and leave him. The rejection and hurt that George will feel affects all the spheres of George's being and will be felt mainly in Tiph-Ereth, his centre (heartache). Remember that all the spheres except Malchuth are connected to Tiph-Ereth and when his loved ones are removed from Malchuth (his external world), all his thoughts and feelings will be directed towards Tiph-Ereth.

Compare this to an elastic band that stretches between Netzach (feelings) and Hod (thoughts). Imagine this band stretching tighter and tighter until it finally snaps. The resultant sting is felt in Tiph-Ereth.

George now has the opportunity to go through the Veil and start examining what lies above. He may decide to avoid facing the facts by keeping Malchuth (his external world) filled with activity and people; or by spending time alone, reaching into Tiph-Ereth, he can start to prioritise his life, acknowledging that his jealousy has created this situation as an opportunity for him to learn about love.

# The negative veils

Above the first sphere, Kether, there are three veils. These are known as the Veils of Negative Existence and they are named as follows:

| | | |
|---|---|---|
| Ayin | Nothing | Universal Spirit |
| Ayin Soph | Nothing Becomes | Universal Will |
| Ayin Soph Aur | Nothing Is | Universal Love |

# The four Qabalistic worlds

The numbered spheres are divided into four worlds. These connect to the 'Holy name' (Tetragrammaton) as mentioned in Chapter 1. Diagram 2.2 shows these worlds. They are as follows:

1. **ATZILUTH** is the first world and consists of Kether and Chockmah. This world is represented by the Yud ( י ), fire (△) and creative energy.

2. **BRIAH** is the second world and consists of Binah. This world is represented by the first He ( ה ), water (▽) and receptive energy.

3. **YETZIRAH** is the third world and consists of Chesed, Geburah, Tiph-Ereth, Netzach, Hod and Yesod. This world is represented by the Vav ( ו ), air (△) and formative energy.

4. **ASSIAH** is the fourth world and consists of Malchuth. This world is represented by the second He ( ה ), earth (▽) and material energy.

Referring back to the mystical story told in Chapter 1, the following connections can be made:

- **Atziluth** is the creative energy that brought the creation of all that is. It is composed of Kether (the loving, light-filled being – the crown) and Chockmah (the male counterpart – universal will and power).

- **Briah** (universal love and understanding) is receptive energy that came about as a result of the first energy. Both of these are above the Abyss and therefore appear very clouded.

- **Yetzirah** (soul and personality) is the formative energy that is the result of the first two energies in a reverse state. Almost like

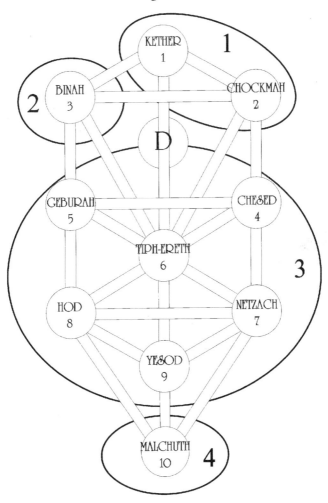

Diagram 2.2: The four Qabalistic worlds

the wine-maker, the grapes and the wine.  The wine does not resemble the wine-maker, nor the grapes, but instead is the result of the efforts of the wine-maker and the qualities of the grapes.

- **Assiah** (the body) is the material, formative energy that springs from the combining of the creative energy with the receptive energy (the recipient of the creativity).

# The connecting paths

Every numbered sphere is connected to other numbered spheres by paths.  The paths that connect the spheres relate to the relationship between the quality of the two specific spheres. For example, Chesed is love and Netzach is feelings. The path that connects these two spheres (path 21) shows the relationship between love and feelings. This path does not include the feelings that are stimulated as a result of the past, which falls on path 28.

Diagram 2.3 and Table 2.2 show the paths in the Tree of Life.  There are 10 numbered spheres and the first path is therefore numbered 11. There are 22 paths in total, corresponding to the 22 letters of the Hebrew alphabet (the Aleph Beth – see Chapter 6) and the 22 cards of the Major Arcana in the Tarot (see Chapter 5).

Table 2.2: Paths and the spheres they connect

| | | | |
|---|---|---|---|
| 11 | Kether – Chockmah | 22 | Geburah – Tiph-Ereth |
| 12 | Kether – Binah | 23 | Geburah – Hod |
| 13 | Kether – Tiph-Ereth | 24 | Tiph-Ereth – Netzach |
| 14 | Chockmah – Binah | 25 | Tiph-Ereth – Yesod |
| 15 | Chockmah – Tiph-Ereth | 26 | Tiph-Ereth – Hod |
| 16 | Chockmah – Chesed | 27 | Netzach – Hod |
| 17 | Binah – Tiph-Ereth | 28 | Netzach – Yesod |
| 18 | Binah – Geburah | 29 | Netzach – Malchuth |
| 19 | Chesed – Geburah | 30 | Hod – Yesod |
| 20 | Chesed – Tiph-Ereth | 31 | Hod – Malchuth |
| 21 | Chesed – Netzach | 32 | Yesod – Malchuth |

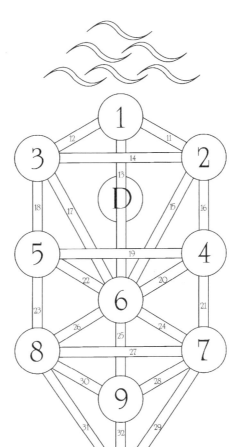

Diagram 2.3: The 22 paths and the Tree of Life

Every sphere and every path has many traditional correspondences, and we will look at some of these later.

# Compile your Tree of Life

You will find it useful to combine everything you have learnt so far on a large diagram. Draw the Tree of Life as explained earlier, mark all the spheres and paths, and write all the corresponding information in the appropriate spaces. Display it where you do your Qabalistic work, to help create constant awareness.

Table 2.3 lists the spheres and their corresponding symbols, colours and equivalents in the physical body. Table 2.4 lists correspondences for the paths. Study both tables carefully, then transfer the information to your Tree of Life.

Table 2.3: The spheres and their correspondences

| No. | Sphere | Colour | Symbol | Body area |
|---|---|---|---|---|
| 1 | Kether | white | swastika | above head |
| 2 | Chockmah | grey | inner robe | left brain |
| 3 | Binah | black | outer robe | right brain |
| D | Daath | lavender | chain | vocal cords |
| 4 | Chesed | blue | sceptre | left shoulder/arm |
| 5 | Geburah | red | spear | right shoulder/arm |
| 6 | Tiph-Ereth | yellow | rosy cross | heart |
| 7 | Netzach | green | girdle | left hip/leg |
| 8 | Hod | orange | spells | right hip/leg |
| 9 | Yesod | purple | sandals, perfumes | genitals |
| 10 | Malchuth | red, green, blue, black | circle | feet/anus |

Table 2.4: The paths and their correspondences

| No. | Hebrew | Colour | Symbol | Body area |
|---|---|---|---|---|
| 11 | Aleph | sky blue | fan | total centre column |
| 12 | Beth | purple | caduceus | right eye |
| 13 | Gimel | silver | bow | left eye |
| 14 | Daleth | midnight blue | girdle | right ear |
| 15 | He | light blue | starcharts | right hand |
| 16 | Vav | indigo | sweat | left hand |
| 17 | Zain | mauve | tripod | right leg |

| 18 | Cheth | maroon | furnace | left leg |
| 19 | Teth | deep purple | heart | right kidney |
| 20 | Yud | slate grey | wand | left kidney |
| 21 | Kaph | dark blue | sceptre | left ear |
| 22 | Lamed | blue | cross | liver |
| 23 | Mem | sea green | wine | left column |
| 24 | Nun | brown | poison | spleen |
| 25 | Samech | yellow | arrow | gall bladder |
| 26 | Ayin | black | lamp | stomach |
| 27 | Pe | bright red | sword | right nostril |
| 28 | Tzaddi | red | burin | intestines |
| 29 | Qoph | yellow-brown | mirror | stomach |
| 30 | Resh | golden yellow | talismans | left nostril |
| 31 | Shin | royal purple | pyramid | right column |
| 32 | Tav | amber | shadow | mouth |

The symbols associated with Yesod (the subconscious) are sandals and perfumes. Reflexology (sandals) and aromatherapy (perfumes) are well known as two alternative healing methods that work on stored emotions in the subconscious.

The body correspondences given above are slightly different from those given on pages 38–39, under the Hebrew Aleph Beth. Both these lists are valid and have been included to give the reader the freedom of choice.

## Exercise 2
## Centring yourself

Belief systems, past experiences, opinions, scepticism and other factors often interfere with our day-to-day living. The following exercise will help you get in touch with the uncomplicated self. Follow the steps carefully. It may be advisable to record this exercise on tape and then play it back.

1. Do the Qabalistic Cross Exercise (Exercise 1, Chapter 1).
2. Make yourself comfortable in a sitting position and close your eyes. Allow your breathing to flow into a pattern without forcing it.

3. Spend a few moments breathing in and out while you allow all the tension in your body to flow into the floor beneath you. Make sure that you are not touching another living being (human, animal or plant).

4. Become aware of who you are, where you are, and why you are about to perform this exercise.

5. Imagine yourself sitting inside a brown bubble, feeling the stillness. Become aware of all five senses and spend some time really getting in touch with each of them. This is the world of Malchuth.

6. Now step out of the bubble and allow all your senses to remain behind. See the brown bubble in front of you containing all five senses.

7. Move yourself inside another bubble, this time a purple one. Become aware of your emotions by allowing your thoughts to drift to past experiences. Emotions are stimulated by an outside force, so you may like to recall a song, smell or the face of a person with whom you have had a relationship.

8. Now step out of the bubble leaving all your emotions behind. Clearly see the purple bubble containing your emotions and the brown one holding all five senses in front of you.

9. Yet again, move yourself into another bubble, this time an orange one. Become aware of all your thoughts and allow them to accumulate and grow. This is the world of Hod.

10. Step out of the bubble, leaving all your thoughts behind. See this orange bubble in front of you holding all your thoughts, the purple one all your emotions, and the brown one all your sensations.

11. For the last time, move into a green bubble and become aware of all your feelings. Pure feelings come from inside and should therefore not be confused with emotions that you have already stored in the purple bubble.

12. Step out of this bubble leaving all your feelings behind. Then clearly see before you the green bubble with your feelings, the orange one with your thoughts, the purple one with your emotions, and the brown one with your sensations.

13. Now repeat the following slowly to yourself:
    - I am a pure soul that has chosen these four vehicles of expression to assist me on all levels of my life.
    - I choose to use any one of these vehicles at any time, should I so desire.
    - I choose to distance myself from any one of these vehicles, should I so desire.
14. Realise the truth in these statements and bring your awareness back to the present.

# 3

# The physical correlation

God created man in His own image, in the image of God
He created him; male and female He created them.

Genesis 1: 27

*T*he word chakra *is Sanskrit for 'wheel' – a 'wheel' of energy within
the body. Chakras are often indicated by a disc, lotus or ball.
They rotate in all directions and vibrate to a certain frequency.*

*There are seven major chakras. These are situated on the spine at
various levels. The spinal column represents the entire body, with the
mind and the spirit intertwining this column. The spine can be compa
red to an electrical current and the chakras to the power points. The
endocrine glands secrete hormones that regulate all the major
functions. These hormones are affected by the mental and emotional
states as well as by diet and environment. Every major chakra is linked
to an endocrine gland and the spine serves as the channel through
which these energies are transported (see Table 3.1).*

Table 3.1: The chakras

| Name | Colour | Sound | Centre | Position | Glands |
|---|---|---|---|---|---|
| Muladhara (root/base) | Red | *LAM* | Physical energy, vitality | Base of spine | Testes/ ovaries (genitals) |
| Svadisthana (sacral) | Orange | *VAM* | Desire, emotions, creativity, sexuality | 5 cm above base of spine | Adrenals (kidneys) |

| Manipura (solar plexus) | Yellow | *RAM* | Personal power, vitality | On spine behind navel | Pancreas (liver) |
|---|---|---|---|---|---|
| Anahata (heart) | Green | *YAM* | Compassion, love | On spine behind chest | Thymus (heart) |
| Vishuddi (throat) | Blue | *HAM* | Communication | On spine behind throat | Thyroid (larynx) |
| Ajna (third eye /brow) | Indigo | *OHM* | Psychic power, higher intuition | Behind space between eyebrows | Pituitary (optic chiasma) |
| Sahasrara (crown) | Violet | *SOHAM* | Spirituality, enlightenment | Hovering above crown of head | Pineal (brain) |

# How do the chakras fit into the Tree?

The Tree of Life can be divided vertically into eight layers. If the two central ones are combined, the resulting seven layers correspond to the seven chakras, as shown below and in Diagram 3.1.

| Spheres | Chakra |
|---|---|
| Kether | Sahasrara |
| Binah, Chockmah | Ajna |
| Daath | Vishuddi |
| Geburah, Chesed, Tiph-Ereth | Anahata |
| Hod, Netzach | Manipura |
| Yesod | Svadisthana |
| Malchuth | Muladhara |

Diagram 3.1 shows that Kether, Daath, Yesod and Malchuth are the only spheres not sharing a chakra with another sphere. Their chakras (Sahasrara, Vishuddi, Svadisthana and Muladhara) are all directly related to the balance between inner and outer.

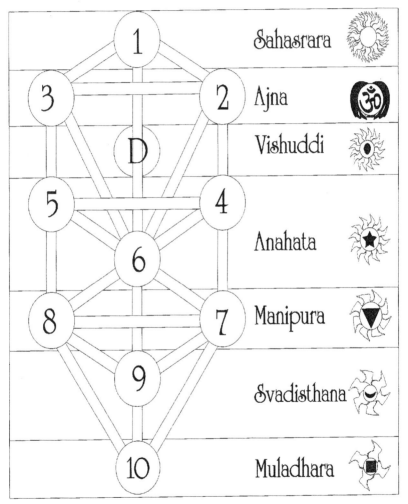

Diagram 3.1: The chakras and the spheres of the Tree of Life

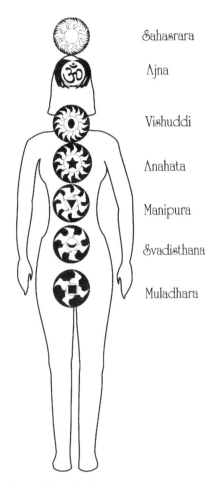

Diagram 3.2: The body and the chakras

- **Sahasrara–Kether** is concerned with the relationship between the inner and outer selves, i.e. the spiritual balance. This chakra can be stimulated by visualising blood pulsing at the top of the head and a violet light entering at the same spot. The sound S-O-H-A-M can be used, aloud or imagined.

- **Vishuddi–Daath** is concerned with communication with the outside world, i.e. the effect that our words have on others. This chakra can be stimulated by visualising blood pulsing in the brain while the light turns to indigo. The sound O-H-M should also be made, aloud or imagined.
- **Svadisthana–Yesod** is concerned with sexual relationships. It is also the balance between the past and the future, which very often depends on the present. This chakra can be stimulated by creating a feeling of being sexually turned-on, the colour orange and the sound V-A-M.
- **Muladhara–Malchuth** is concerned with survival in this world and how the outside world affects the inner world through the senses. This chakra can be stimulated by concentrating on contracting the anus, the colour red and the sound L-A-M.

Diagram 3.1 also shows that the pairs Binah and Chockmah and Hod and Netzach, each relate to single chakras. These chakras (Ajna and Manipura) are all related to inner balance. Both these chakras will be functional even when the inner balance is distorted.

- **Ajna–Binah–Chockmah** is concerned with the inner balance between spiritual love and will, which brings about psychic abilities. This chakra can be stimulated by concentrating on the pulsations in the brain behind the forehead, the colour indigo and the sound O-H-M.
- **Manipura–Netzach–Hod** is concerned with the inner balance of thoughts and feelings. This chakra can be stimulated by concentrating on absorbing energy into the solar plexus, the colour yellow and the sound R-A-M.

The only remaining chakra is the Anahata chakra which is associated with Tiph-Ereth, Geburah and Chesed. This chakra will not be functional when there is an imbalance in the spheres.

- **Anahata–Tiph-Ereth–Geburah–Chesed** is concerned with the individual balance between love and will. This chakra can be stimulated by concentrating on your heart pulsating, the colour green and the sound Y-A-M.

# Yoga

Yoga is often perceived as a purely physical exercise. The initial purpose of yoga may be only physical but this is in order to gain control of the physical before one can move on to the mental and spiritual plane. Yoga is in total a system of meditation and self-control designed to produce mystical experiences and spiritual insights.

The Western Tradition is based on theory, proven by tests and then accumulated into statistical data. In the Eastern Tradition a student accepts nothing as true unless it is experienced as a personal truth. Yoga provides the student with the opportunity to release excess intellectual, emotional and physical energy in an individual, harmonious fashion.

# Kundalini

There are seven schools of yoga that originate from the Eastern disciplines. One of these schools of yoga is called Laya yoga and its two main features are the chakras and the Kundalini. Kundalini is described as an energy, like a coiled-up snake, that lies dormant in the base chakra. This energy is alive and blocks the channel up the spine through the other six chakras.

The purpose of practising Laya yoga is to awaken the Kundalini. This energy will then rise and move upwards through the other six chakras bringing with it the life-force. This energy is most commonly directed outwards, during orgasm. The Kundalini lies in the Muladhara (root/base) chakra and orgasm happens in the Svadisthana (sacral) chakra, which means that she rises only for a short distance. Through the practice of Laya yoga, this force can be lifted all the way up to the Sahasrara (crown) chakra.

The spine and the Kundalini together form a union of all opposites. The spine (symbolically the pole, straight) is dead and the Kundalini (symbolically the snake, coiled) is alive. The spine is called the 'axis of Creation' and serves as a tube (channel) on which the chakras are threaded (very much as on a string of beads). Another two channels,

one feminine (Yin) and one masculine (Yang) thread their way up around the centre by swinging from left to right.

Once the yogi has wilfully awakened the Kundalini, she rises step by step through the chakras. The chakras turn on the centre channel while the Yin and Yang channels change position, which in turn renders them latent. This latency is again reactivated, this time also enlightened by the power received from the crown chakra, by the Kundalini on her return to the base chakra. Once the Kundalini returns to its slumber, the ego is pulled down into its origin, the Muladhara chakra. Diagram 3.3 shows the Kundalini, also known as the Caduceus.

# Colours

When working with the chakras, colour becomes very important. A popular alternative healing method available today is 'colour therapy'. The colours used in this therapy can often be traced back to the chakras and the spheres on the Tree of Life. Table 3.2 compares the different colours.

Table 3.2: Chakra and sphere colours

| Chakra colour | Chakra name | Sphere name | Sphere colour |
| --- | --- | --- | --- |
| Violet | Sahasrara | Kether (1) | Brilliant white |
| Indigo | Ajna | Chockmah (2) | Grey |
| | | Binah (3) | Black |
| Blue | Vishuddi | Daath | Lavender |
| Green | Anahata | Chesed (4) | Blue |
| | | Geburah (5) | Red |
| | | Tiph-Ereth (6) | Yellow |
| Yellow | Manipura | Netzach (7) | Emerald green |
| | | Hod (8) | Orange |
| Orange | Svadisthana | Yesod (9) | Violet |
| Red | Muladhara | Malchuth (10) | Russet, olive, citrine, black |

Diagram 3.3: The Kundalini and the Tree of Life

The colours of the chakras do not always correspond with the colours of the spheres. However, both these systems can be used in colour therapy. At the end of this chapter is a healing meditation where colours will be used.

# The Tree of Life and the Body

Table 3.3 shows the spheres and paths with their associated body parts, disorders and colours. It may help you to memorise body parts if you stand against a life-size Tree of Life.

Table 3.3: Spheres, paths and associated disorders and colours

| Sphere /path | Body part | Disease | Colour |
| --- | --- | --- | --- |
| 1 | Not in body | Death | Brilliant white |
| 2 | Left brain | Insanity | Grey |
| 3 | Right brain | Loss of memory | Black |
| D | Vocal cords | Loss of soul | Lavender |
| 4 | Left shoulder and arm | Dropsy | Blue |
| 5 | Right shoulder and arm | Fever | Red |
| 6 | Heart and lungs | Heart diseases | Yellow/gold |
| 7 | Left hip and leg | Skin problems | Green |
| 8 | Right hip and leg | Nerves problems | Orange |
| 9 | Genitals | Impotency | Purple |
| 10 | Feet/anus | Sterility | Russet, olive, black and citrine |
| 11 | Respiratory organs | Fluxes | Sky blue |
| 12 | Nervous system | Ataxia | Purple |
| 13 | Lymphatic system | Mentrual problems | Silver |
| 14 | Genital system | Sexual diseases | Midnight blue |
| 15 | Head and face | Cystitis | Light blue |
| 16 | Shoulders and arms | Indigestion | Deep blue |
| 17 | Lungs | Pneumonia | Mauve |
| 18 | Stomach | Rheumatism | Maroon |
| 19 | Heart | Heart diseases | Deep purple |
| 20 | Spine | Spinal disorders | Slate grey |
| 21 | Digestive system | Gout | Dark blue |
| 22 | Liver | Kidney disorders | Blue |
| 23 | Nutritional organs | Chill | Sea green |
| 24 | Intestines | Cancer | Brown |
| 25 | Hips and thighs | Thrombosis | Yellow |

| 26 | Genital system | Arthritis | Black |
| 27 | Muscular system | Inflammation | Bright red |
| 28 | Kidneys and bladder | Apoplexy | Red |
| 29 | Legs and feet | Gout | Dull yellow |
| 30 | Circulatory system | Repletion | Golden yellow |
| 31 | Intelligence | Insanity | Royal purple |
| 32 | Skeleton | Arteriosclerosis | Amber |

The information in Table 3.3 can be transferred onto the Tree of Life. When you wear clothes with the appropriate colour, the various spheres and paths will be stimulated and 'colour therapy' will be applied.

Diagram 3.4 shows the body with the Tree of Life overlapping it.

# Diseases and the Tree of Life

As discussed in Chapter 2, Daath is the gateway to the reverse side of the Tree of Life (the Tree of Evil). Table 3.4 shows the opposites involved in these two trees:

Table 3.4: The Tree of Life and the Tree of Evil

| Tree of Life | No. | Tree of Evil |
| --- | --- | --- |
| Light | 0 | Darkness |
| Pure spirit | 1 | Atheism |
| Wisdom | 2 | Stupidity |
| Understanding | 3 | Antipathy |
| Experience | D | Ignorance |
| Compassion | 4 | Apathy |
| Discipline | 5 | Cruelty |
| Beauty and harmony | 6 | Ugliness |
| Achievement | 7 | Lust |
| Glory | 8 | Greed |
| Foundation of life | 9 | Instability |
| External world | 10 | Materialism |

All the spheres on the central column have the same dark and light sides as a full moon. The spheres on the right (often termed the positive side) and the ones on the left (often termed the negative side) have duplicates on the evil side of the Tree of Life.  Do not

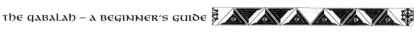

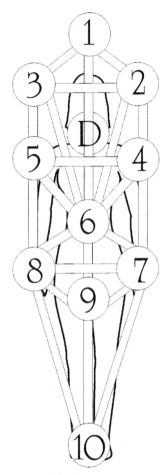

Diagram 3.4: The body and the Tree of Life

confuse this with dark and light, often used instead of positive and negative. A three-dimensional image of the Tree of Life, Diagram 3.5, will help you to understand this concept.

Both positives and negatives have their own positives and negatives; positive positive, negative positive, negative negative and positive negative. All humans have these positives and negatives. It is

important to recognise the dark side within. Only then can one choose to live in the light where ignorance is no excuse.

Try to imagine how difficult it would be to fight an unknown enemy. His hiding place could be anywhere and he could strike without warning.

Daath is the gate to these dark sides of the spheres. On these dark sides lie all the demons and vices. When a sphere is not inhabited

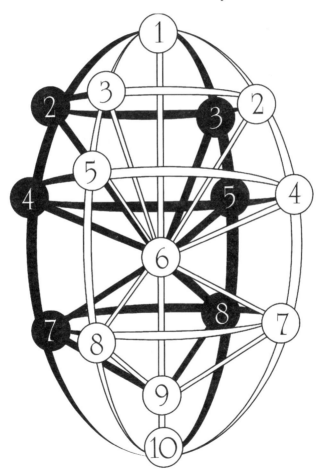

Diagram 3.5: The three-dimensional Tree of Life

by the light, the demons will occupy it and manifest on the physical body in the appropriate sphere.

Try comparing this principle with a house; when there is no paying tenant occupying this house, the creatures of the night will move in. These creatures hang around in the shadows (Abyss) at the gate to the suburb (Daath), observing the movement in the house and waiting for the right moment.

These creatures of the night often test the territory before they finally move in. It is therefore important to listen to your body. The first signs of illness are often preceded by a gentle warning whisper. If you learn to recognise the whisper, the shout will not be necessary.

# Psychological connection to the Tree

The Oxford dictionary states that a psychosomatic illness is one caused or aggravated by mental stress; an illness that involves both the mind and the body. The mind is a very powerful instrument and should therefore be looked at more closely.

There are four different levels of awareness and they fit into the Tree of Life as shown in Table 3.5.

Table 3.5: Levels of awareness

| Mind | Wave | Hz | Associated spheres |
|---|---|---|---|
| Conscious | Beta | 150–15 | Malchuth (10)<br>Hod (8)<br>Netzach (7) |
| Subconscious | Alpha | 15–5 | Yesod (9) |
| Unconscious | Theta | 7–3 | Tiph-Ereth (6)<br>Geburah (5)<br>Chesed (4) |
| Higher-conscious | Delta | 3–0 | Binah (3)<br>Chockmah (2)<br>Kether (1) |

- The **conscious** state (Beta brain waves) is that during which awareness of what is happening through the senses, thoughts and feelings is active. This is the everyday, awake and alert state.
- The **subconscious** state (Alpha brain waves) is the one during which all the senses, thoughts and feelings are shut-off. This state is achieved just prior to falling asleep and when entering a state of meditation.
- The **unconscious** state (Theta brain waves) is the state during which the part of the mind that is not normally accessible to consciousness but which is found to affect behaviour, is active. This state is achieved when falling asleep and losing total awareness of the surroundings.
- The **higher conscious** (Delta brain waves) is the God-spark in all. This state is only sometimes accessible through a very deep sleep. Dreams occur when moving from the Delta to Theta waves and these dreams are remembered once Alpha waves is entered. Dreams are very often forgotten once Beta waves have taken over.

These various levels of brain waves are indicated in Diagram 3.6. Note how similar these are to the auric fields in Diagram 3.7.

# The aura and the physical body

There is an electromagnetic field that surrounds the physical body. This field is known as the aura and has been recorded by a technique called Kirlian photography. By training oneself, it is possible to see auras with the physical eye. There are many in-depth studies available that teach various techniques.

The aura dies prior to the death of the body. Some believe that the aura leaves the body up to 40 hours prior to physical death. Contemplate then the following: if an aeroplane crashes and all passengers are killed in the accident, would they then have boarded the aeroplane without their auras? Imagine the dynamics involved here.

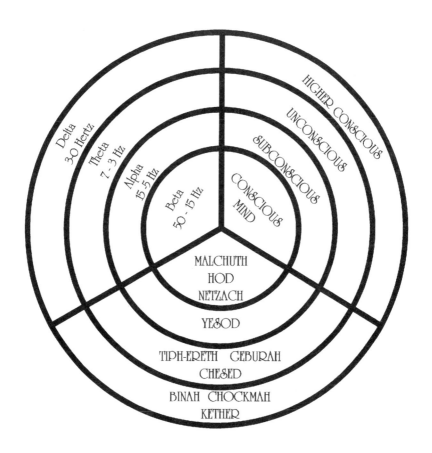

Diagram 3.6: The levels of awareness

In Chapter 2, after connecting all the spheres in numerical order, we saw how the 'Flash of Creation' was created. This started with the spirit, then created the soul and only then the personality and the body. This indicates that the soul, personality and body only manifest as a result of the spirit. Looking at the Flash of Creation in reverse, the following can be said:

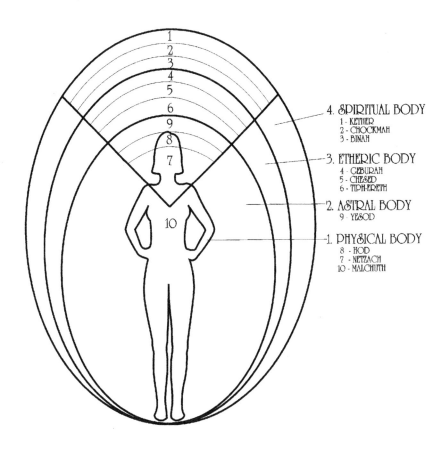

4. SPIRITUAL BODY
1 - KETHER
2 - CHOCKMAH
3 - BINAH

3. ETHERIC BODY
4 - GEBURAH
5 - CHESED
6 - TIPH-ERETH

2. ASTRAL BODY
9 - YESOD

1. PHYSICAL BODY
8 - HOD
7 - NETZACH
10 - MALCHUTH

Diagram 3.7: The auric fields

- The first body is the physical one, which is equivalent to the conscious mind and Malchuth (10), Hod (8) and Netzach (7).
- The second body is the astral one, which is equivalent to the subconscious mind and Yesod (9).

- The third body is the etheric one, which is equivalent to the unconscious mind and Tiph-Ereth (6), Geburah (5) and Chesed (4).
- The fourth body is the spiritual one, which is equivalent to the higher conscious mind, Binah (3), Chockmah (2) and Kether (1).

It is interesting to note how the aura fits into the various levels of awareness. Note how the three-dimensional Tree of Life (Diagram 3.5) has the same appearance as the aura (Diagram 3.7). It is believed that Buddha's aura could be felt one mile from his physical body. An aura normally extends approximately three metres from the body and is made up of three main layers.

These three layers can be subdivided into another three sub-layers which would then make the aura a nine-layered field. These nine layers, together with the physical body, are the equivalent of the 10 numbered spheres on the Tree of Life. (See Diagram 3.7.)

## EXERCISE 3
## HEALING MEDITATION

Holistic healing is 'whole healing' and, as the name suggests, it includes the whole or complete person, i.e. body, personality, soul, spirit and the relationship with the outer world. The best form of healing is the one performed on the self during which the Tree of Life can be an important instrument allowing healing to take place. The body has been designed to heal itself by regenerating cells to replace damaged ones. This is clearly visible when a knee has been scraped. The blood dries and forms a scab that protects the sore. Healing takes place under this scab and once this has been accomplished, the scab lifts and falls off.

The following healing exercise can be performed anywhere, but if it is at all possible, find a quiet, comfortable spot in the garden under a tree. Have a diagram of the Tree of Life handy and study this, allowing your breathing to form a pattern.

1. Now close your eyes and deepen your breathing. Allow your in-breath to flow automatically into your out-breath thereby connecting your breathing into a continuous flow. Feel the

energy entering your body and running down your spine with every in-breath and then feel the energy rise up the front of your body and leave it with every out-breath.

2. Imagine yourself sitting/lying with the diagram of the Tree of Life inscribed over your body while taking particular notice of the spheres on the centre pillar, i.e. Malchuth, Yesod, Tiph-Ereth, Daath and Kether. Feel these spheres as vortexes on your spine and the energy whirling around filling every part with health and energy. Take special note of areas that may need a little more energy and then allow this stream to linger a little longer in those areas.

3. Now become aware of the spheres on the right column, i.e. Hod, Geburah and Binah, and then those on the left column, i.e. Netzach, Chesed and Chockmah. Now feel the energy change direction: instead of it rising up the front of your body, allow it to split into two equal streams and flow up the left and right of your body. Feel the spheres of the side columns as vortexes and, as before, allow the energy to whirl around while filling every part with health and energy. Allow the energy more time in areas that are particularly out of balance.

4. Notice how certain areas are full of discomfort, whether from tension or pain. Allow this discomfort to dissolve into the energy just as ink dissipates in water and then just let it go with your next out-breath. Continue this until all discomfort has left your body.

5. When you are ready, allow your breathing to return to normal, notice the surface on which you are sitting and bring your awareness back to your environment. Open your eyes and realise that the healing you apply to yourself is at the same time healing the whole universe.

# CHAPTER 4

# ANGELS AND ARCHANGELS

*By* now you should have some grasp of the Tree of Life and to the physical and psychological bodies. We will now take a different approach to the Tree in order to understand the Angels, Archangels and God-Forces.

Allow the Tree of Life to become a road map showing the route from the present position (Malchuth) to an end destination (Kether) while travelling through various towns (all other spheres). This map will be one of light and love. The end destination (Kether) lies on the top of a very high mountain and in order to reach this level of understanding the awareness needs to be lifted with every step. There are lessons to be found along the way that will make the journey a more joyous one.

Every town on this journey will provide the opportunity to overcome an obstacle and to uncover a very special gift that will offer assistance on the journey. The further away from Malchuth, the more meaningful the messages become. It is important to realise that the human body is the soul's home during this lifetime and that all spiritual experiences should therefore be useful and adaptable to each individual reality.

If you use your imagination, you will be able to visualise each town on the journey as holding within its centre a round, colourful temple where the God-Forces, Archangels and Angels live. These entities have wisdom, love and power and they are lovingly willing to help on the journey of self-development. All that is needed is to evoke these qualities and then to carry them into the physical realm.

Diagram 4.1 provides a visual image of this journey.

# malchuth

This is the town in which we spend most of our waking hours. It is the level that affects daily life most directly and it is therefore very

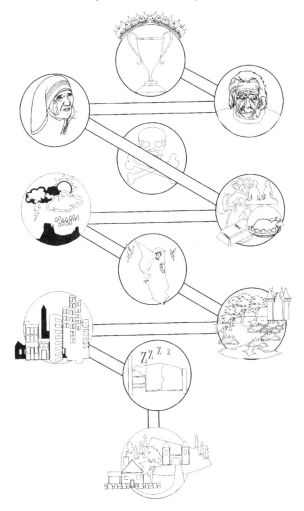

Diagram 4.1: The angelic journey

important to realise that whatever we learn on this journey needs to be channelled back to Malchuth.

Residing within the colourful temple of Malchuth is the Order of Blessed Souls. They are the saints that take care of the devas on the earth plane. The Archangel in charge is Sandlaphon who is known as the Prince of Prayer. He is the one that gathers all our prayers and delivers them to the King of Kings. He is also in charge of all embryos and the determination of their sex. Above him is Adonai Ha-Aretz, Lord of Earth and the Visible Universe.

The obstacles to overcome on this level are inertia (slowness in acting) and avarice (greed for gain), and the special gift to be uncovered is discrimination. It is important to learn how to discriminate between good and bad, when to act, when to hold back, when to gain and when to let go. The Order of Blessed Souls will offer assistance with any difficulty that may be experienced when discrimination is called for.

## yesod

The next town on the map is Yesod. Here understanding of the universe and all its cycles can be increased. Past and future lives are recorded on this level and these records are taken care of by the angels of Yesod who are known as the Angels of Light and Glory, and the Keepers of the Akashic Records. Before studying any of these records it is necessary to ask the permission of the angels.

Gabriel is the Archangel in charge of the Angels, and he is the Archangel of Truth. He is the chief of the guards placed over Paradise. Yesod is the gateway to all other levels of awareness. Gabriel brings the gift of hope and above him is Shaddai El Chai or the Almighty Living God. Touching this God-Force one may experience the 'Vision of the Machinery of the Universe'.

The obstacles that need to be overcome on this level are idleness and stagnation and the special gift that can be uncovered is independence. Independence within and without can be better understood once the past and the future are realised. Knowing the

plan behind all will be revealed when dependence upon the reasons for the plan is no longer needed.

## hod

The town of Hod is filled with libraries, communication networks, industry, trade and commerce. This is the level where, learning how to use the mind and how to imprint the will upon the astral matters, you may obtain greater manifestations in the physical world.

Residing within the temple of Hod is the God-Force known as Elohim Tzaboath, which means God of Hosts Ruling the Universe in Wisdom and Harmony. The Archangel of Hod is Michael, Prince of Splendour and Wisdom, and he teaches patience. Working under him are the Beni Elohim, or the Sons of God, and they are the transmitters of divine consciousness into the mind through gaining greater knowledge.

The obstacles that need to be overcome on this level are falsehood, dishonesty and mental rigidity, while the special gift to be uncovered is truthfulness. Knowledge gives greater awareness, which in turn eliminates dishonesty, thereby strengthening individual truth. Patience is an asset when gaining knowledge and this quality can be learned from Michael.

## NETZACH

Netzach is a beautiful town filled with emerald-green hills, plants and fairies. Inner sanctuaries are located in Netzach. This is where inspiration, creativity and the deeper meanings in our relationships can be found.

In the castle of Netzach is the God-Force Jehovah Tzaboath, or the God of Hosts, who offers assistance in recognising and expressing feelings in a positive manner. Haniel is the Archangel active on this level and she is the Archangel of Love and Harmony. She advises us on our creativity. Working under her are the Elohim or Gods/ Goddesses. They keep an eye on the religious leaders and help them make the correct decisions.

The obstacle to overcome here is lust, and the special gift to uncover is unselfishness. Feelings and higher emotions can be used in a good, unselfish way or in a bad, lustful way. With the assistance of the entities, feelings can be recognised and then expressed in an unconditional way.

## Tiph-Ereth

Tiph-Ereth is reached halfway along the journey. This town has a beautiful, radiant, golden sun and everything takes on a golden tint. This is a very exciting 'pit-stop' and a little more time should be spent on this level of awareness.

The castle of Tiph-Ereth is special because Guardian Angels and Healing Angels reside here as well. During the exercise at the end of this chapter you will meet your Guardian Angel. The God-Force at this level is Jehovah Aloah va Daath, or the God of Knowledge and Wisdom. Raphael is the Archangel active here and he is often referred to as the Angel of Brightness, Beauty, Healing and Life. Raphael is the Healing Angel and he offers assistance in directing any kind of healing. Working under him are the Malachim, who are known as the Angelic Kings. They are the ones that bring miracles upon the earth.

The obstacles to overcome on this level are false pride and selfishness, while the special gift to uncover is devotion to the Great Work. Only by letting go of false pride and selfish ways can we realise that beauty is within all, and that everyone forms part of the Great Work.

## Geburah

Geburah is a powerful town filled with energy and courage. All the natural forces, the understanding of their uses, individual capabilities of controlling these and the responsibility thereof are located on this level.

Residing in the castle of Geburah is the God-Force Elohim Gibor, which means God Almighty and who removes powers when they are

no longer useful while making space for new ones. The Archangel active on this level is Kamael, or the Prince of Strength and Courage, and he protects the weak. Working under him are the Seraphim, or the Flaming Ones, who offer assistance in protecting the self from others wishing harm.

The obstacles to overcome on this level are cruelty and restriction while the special gifts to uncover are energy and courage. All the natural forces are available and when using them with cruelty, restriction is created.

## chesed

The town Chesed is filled with abundance and unconditional love. This is the level at which the lesson about the true power of love and how to use it to reach for the stars is available.

In the castle of Chesed is the God-Force El, or simply God, the Mighty One. Under Him is the Archangel Tzadkiel, who is called the Prince of Mercy and Beneficence, and who was the protecting Angel of Abraham. Tzadkiel is in charge of an order of Angels called the Brilliant Ones, sometimes referred to as the Dominations. These Angels are responsible for the greatness of God being manifested in individual lives.

The obstacles that need to be overcome on this level are bigotry and hypocrisy, while the special gift to uncover is obedience. Obedience to the self creates freedom and power in the physical and spiritual and once this reality is experienced, sacrificing on the physical level becomes secondary.

## daath

On the road between Chesed and Binah is a lavender town in the distance. This town is Daath, and it is not accessible from the road. It should not be explored until this journey has been completed.

## BINAh

Binah is a town filled with understanding. It holds within its borders all the understanding of situations that cause confusion in Malchuth. The colour of the temple of Binah is black, which is the only colour that holds all other colours.

The God-Force that resides in this black temple is Jehovah Elohim and He takes care of the perfection of the creation. Under Him we will find Archangel Tzaphkiel, who is called the Prince of Spiritual Strife against Evil. He helps with understanding difficult confrontations and how to overcome them. He is in charge of the Aralim Angels, sometimes called the Strong and Mighty Ones, and they offer help to hold on long enough to achieve understanding.

The obstacles to overcome on this level are avarice and greed and the special gift to uncover is silence. Silence is necessary when understanding is needed and when avoiding this silence, greed steps in creating a need to cling to things.

## chockmah

Chockmah is a town filled with wisdom in its purest form. It is at this level that things can be put into motion. The colour of the temple of Chockmah is grey, which is a mixture of the black of Binah and the brilliant white of Kether.

The God-Force that is at this level is Yah, which means Divine, and under Him is the Archangel Ratziel, the Prince of Knowledge of Hidden and Concealed Things. Ratziel reveals to us the greater wisdom of the workings of the universe and what lies behind it all. He is in charge of the Auphanim Angels who are also called the Whirling Forces. They will reveal a vision of God. It is said that God may not be seen face to face, but this vision alone is powerful enough to instil a devotion.

There are no more obstacles at this level, and the special gift that can be uncovered is Devotion to the Great Work. The powerful experience of seeing the vision of God face to face awakens this

incredible devotion that allows the individual to apply the wisdom of Chockmah in Malchuth.

## KETHER

Kether is the final destination and the brilliance of this level can only be experienced once all the other levels have been worked through. Kether is the level filled with inspirations, ideas, and conceptions that reach far into the future.

The temple of Kether is brilliant white and the God-Force that resides within this temple is Eheieh, which is the name that was given to Moses by God on Mount Sinai when he received the Ten Commandments. The Archangel Metatron works on this level and His task is to reveal the Qabalah once the awareness is acute enough to accept it. Under him are the Chaioth ha-Qadesh, the Holy Living Creatures who are the Angels of Love, Light and Fire. They offer the understanding that is needed to use the Qabalah in spiritual evolution.

There are no obstacles on this level, and the special gift to uncover is the Attainment and Completion of the Great Work. Note that Tiph-Ereth, Chockmah and Kether are the only three spheres that have a special gift connected with the Great Work. This ties in with the mystical story told in Chapter 1.

## EXERCISE 4
## YOUR GUARDIAN ANGEL

Sit or lie in a comfortable position and close your eyes. Allow your breathing to fall into a rhythm without any force. Be aware of your thoughts, feelings and body without hanging on to any of them. Just allow them to come and then let them go.

1. Now imagine yourself walking towards your inner sanctuary, that place where you feel completely safe and secure, the most beautiful place in the world for you. Feel the grass under your feet; smell the flowers around you; hear the wind blowing

through the trees; feel the sun shine on your face. Spend some time in your inner sanctuary and explore a little.

2. When you are ready, look around until you find a bench under a tree. This bench may be any shape, any colour and made from anything you wish. Walk towards the bench, sit or lie down and make yourself comfortable. Allow all the elements of nature around you to continue at their own pace and rhythm and become part of them. Just simply be.

3. Now become aware of a presence behind you. This presence is your Guardian Angel. You may see, feel, hear, smell or simply sense your Guardian Angel. Whichever way you experience the presence, this is the way it is meant to be for you. Allow this presence to enfold you and notice the incredible love within it.

4. When you are ready you may wish to turn around and look at your Angel. Your Angel may be a man, woman, child, animal, only a colour, smell, light; anything that feels right for you. Do not judge the image of your Guardian Angel, but instead accept it with all its love and care.

5. Explore by talking with your Guardian Angel. Ask his/her/its advice about a difficult situation that you may be experiencing at this stage in your life. Your conversation may be verbal or non-verbal. Ask your Angel for his/her/its name. This name is your secret. Never reveal it to anyone: save it for when you need to call on your Guardian Angel.

6. The advice that your Guardian Angel gives you should always be of a positive nature and be an expansion and extension of your life. Use all the spheres in the Tree of Life to check the validity of this advice.

7. When you are ready, bring your consciousness back to your surroundings and allow your body to feel the surface on which you are sitting or lying. When you are ready, open your eyes and either draw a picture or write a few sentences about your experience.

8. It is important that you ground yourself, i.e. use Malchuth and the energy of this experience in order to use the information gained.

# 5

# THE TAROT AND THE TREE OF LIFE

*The Tarot is in a nutshell a set of 78 cards that contain various universal symbols incorporated into pictures. The Tarot can be used as a divination tool.*

*When exploring the word 'Tarot', the following can be said:*

- Tarot means 'principle, law or essence'.
- Taro means 'wheeling essence'.
- Rota means 'essential wheel'.
- Torah means 'essential law'.
- Arcana means 'hidden or mysterious'.

*All these words and their meanings are held within the Tarot.*

*There are many legends connected with the origin of the Tarot. One of these tells how after Moses received the secrets of the Qabalah on Mount Sinai, some of these leaked out to the Egyptians. These secrets were passed on to the Gypsies, who then not only used the Tarot as a basis for the ordinary pack of playing cards as known today, but also spread it through Europe.*

*The symbols of the Tarot can be used to go on a spiritual journey as far or as deep as needed. Symbols are unique to each individual and reflect attitudes and beliefs in life. Your understanding of the cards will only stretch as far as your understanding of life allows. The images contained in the designs are merely mirrors reflecting the inner picture.*

*The age-old saying 'Beauty lies in the eyes of the beholder' plays a strong role in the Tarot cards. Only when there is beauty within can it be recognised in others and when there are fears within, these will*

*create a disharmonious relationship between two people. The Tarot, therefore, indirectly brings to the surface all that lies within the reader.*

*There are currently hundreds of different designs available and selecting the correct one may be time-consuming. However, the time is well spent if it enables a rapport to develop between the reader and the cards.*

*For the purpose of self-development, the Tarot will be used as a means of discovering the beauty and fears within and answers to inner questions. Should the reader wish to take this topic further, an in-depth study should be made.*

# Tbe Tarot and tbe Tree of Life

A Tarot pack consists of 78 cards: 22 Major Arcana and 56 Minor Arcana. These two levels are indeed very different. The Major Arcana are at a much higher level and each of the 22 cards corresponds to one of the 22 paths that connect the spheres on the Tree of Life. The Minor Arcana correspond to the spheres themselves.

Each card has positive and negative aspects. Many interpreters attach negative meanings to a card that appears upside down in a reading. However, positive and negative are present in all human beings, and it is better to explore both aspects of a card, whichever way up it appears.

## Tbe Major Arcana

The 22 cards in the Major Arcana are numbered from 0 to 21 while the paths on the Tree of Life are numbered from 11 to 32. Each card has a number of possible meanings and these will change from time to time within certain limits. The meaning that applies today is directly related to the information needed today. The 22 cards in the Major Arcana can be seen as 22 different aspects of the self.

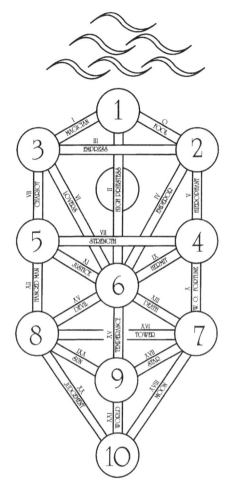

Diagram 5.1: The Major Arcana and the Tree of Life

Table 5.1: The Major Arcana

| Card | Path | Card name | General meaning |
|------|------|-----------|-----------------|
| 0 | 11 | Fool | Extravagance, enthusiasm, carelessness |
| I | 12 | Magician | Skills, diplomacy, communication |
| II | 13 | High Priestess | Mystery, silence, secrets, wisdom |

| III | 14 | Empress | Nature, fertility, initiative |
| IV | 15 | Emperor | Stability, protection, conviction |
| V | 16 | Hierophant | Learning, teaching, inspiration |
| VI | 17 | Lovers | Attraction, beauty, obstacles overcome |
| VII | 18 | Chariot | Trapped situation, help offered |
| VIII | 19 | Strength | Facing inner fears, courage, power |
| IX | 20 | Hermit | Inner search, prudence, disappointment |
| X | 21 | Wheel of Fortune | Taking risks, good luck, success |
| XI | 22 | Justice | Karma, governing, fairness, integrity |
| XII | 23 | Hanged Man | Sacrifice, wisdom, circumspection |
| XIII | 24 | Death | Transformation, ending, total change |
| XIV | 25 | Temperance | Spiritual in physical, inner wisdom |
| XV | 26 | Devil | Entrapment, manipulation, materialism |
| XVI | 27 | Tower | Sudden changes, disruption, confusion |
| XVII | 28 | Star | Fertilisation, new growth, searching |
| XVIII | 29 | Moon | Deception, secrets, danger |
| XIX | 30 | Sun | Contentment, happiness, good marriage |
| XX | 31 | Judgement | Old fears surfacing, karma, new life |
| XXI | 32 | World | Travel, relocation, broader horizon |

Diagram 5.1 shows the Major Arcana and the Tree of Life.

## The Minor Arcana

The Minor Arcana in the Tarot consists of four suits, like the ordinary pack of cards. Each suit consists of ten numbered cards and four Court cards. Each of the four numbered cards corresponds to the individual sphere with the same number, while each of the four Court cards belongs to one of the four worlds in the Tree of Life (Chapter 2).

The four suits of the Minor Arcana correspond to the four elements that are present in all living beings and so do the four Court cards. It also corresponds to the four letters in the name of God, Jehovah (IHVH):

| I | י         | Yud | Fire | Father | Wands | Intuition | King |
| H | ה         | He | Water | Mother | Cups | Feeling | Queen |
| V | ו         | Vav | Air | Son | Swords | Thinking | Knight |
| H | ה         | He | Earth | Daughter | Discs | Sensations | Page |

I suggest that you repeat the exercise at the end of Chapter 2. The four bubbles can now be linked to the four suits of the Minor Arcana.

| Brown | Sensations | Malchuth | Discs/Pentacles |
| Violet | Emotions | Yesod | Wands |
| Orange | Thinking | Hod | Swords |
| Green | Feeling | Netzach | Cups |

Table 5.2 indicates how the Minor Arcana fits into the Tree of Life.

Table 5.2: The Minor Arcana

| Card | Sphere | Overall meaning |
| --- | --- | --- |
| 1 | 1 Kether | New beginnings |
| 2 | 2 Chockmah | Partnership matters |
| King | 2 Chockmah | Mature men, assertion, achievement, material success and stability |
| 3 | 3 Binah | New projects, joint enterprises, optimistic new beginnings |
| Queen | 3 Binah | Mature woman, satisfaction, feminine forms of achievement, comfort |
| 4 | 4 Chesed | Stability, security, putting down roots |
| 5 | 5 Geburah | Loss, sadness, regret, looking backwards, giving up of outworn attitudes, change |
| 6 | 6 Tiph-Ereth | Moving forward in finances and family, travel and taking up new challenges |
| Knight | 6 Tiph-Ereth | Young men, challenges, action in affairs |
| 7 | 7 Netzach | Caution, work, patience, care needed, priorities and values to be worked out |
| 8 | 8 Hod | Expansion of horizons, changes in job, environment or attitude |
| 9 | 9 Yesod | Satisfaction and security, hanging on too tightly |
| 10 | 10 Malchuth | Completion, happiness, achievement, emotional success, joy, heart's desire, security; or total loss and rejection |
| Page | 10 Malchuth | Young woman, child, information |

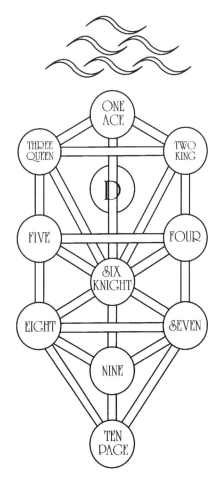

Diagram 5.2: The Minor Arcana and the Tree of Life

From the information in Table 5.2 the following observations can be made:

- Court cards are normally people, or people bringing about situations. King – mature man, masculine energy; Queen – mature woman, feminine energy; Knight – young man, young woman,

movement in affairs; Page – young woman, child, enquiries, information, news.

- The Ace cards are optimistic new beginnings; Pentacles/Discs – Money; Swords – Idea; Cups – Love; Wands – Birth.
- Pentacles/Discs are material matters, earthly goods, money, property, business; all things that we can identify with our senses. Pentacles/Discs Court cards are material, business, banking people.
- Cups are emotional matters, love, hate, worry, sadness, happiness, comfort; all things connected to our inner feelings. Cup Court cards are caring but lazy people.
- Wands are active energies. Negotiations, movement, projects, creativity, hassles; Getting something off the ground or being blocked from doing so. Wand Court cards are exciting people, wasters of energy.
- Swords are thinking matters. Ideas, plotting, planning, worry, fear, loss, achievement, intellect, health. Sword Court cards are professional people, cool and logical or crazy, aggressive, nasty people.

Diagram 5.2 shows the Minor Arcana and the Tree of Life.

# The Tarot and self-development

The Tree of Life as it lies over the body (see Diagram 3.4) clearly shows that when on both our feet (standing still) total balance is achieved. Once walking, the weight is shifted from the right foot/leg to the left foot/leg and movement forward is achieved while the rest of the body remains upright. This shifting also happens on a higher level. In some situations we need to be assertive, in others more flexible. When we choose to shift the awareness from the one side to the other, others are allowed to do the same, and a win–win situation is created.

We can split the Tarot cards into three groups:

- **Major Arcana**: All 22 cards are different facets of the self. Example: When the Hermit steps forward, we find ourselves searching for answers and when the Fool takes his place we feel enthusiastic and energetic.
- **Minor Arcana – Court cards**: These 16 cards are different types of people. This concept is that of Carl Jung, a Swiss psychiatrist who categorised personalities into archetypes. All these archetypes are in the Court cards in all their variations.
- **Minor Arcana – numbered cards**: The 40 cards that fall within this category can be viewed as circumstances at play in the environment. New opportunities come with Aces and completion with tens.

## Get to know your cards

If you attach the complete Tarot pack either on the large map of the Tree of Life or on a wall in the three different groups mentioned above, you can begin to deepen your understanding. You select a card at random every day and make sure that you are familiar with its position on the Tree of Life. Carry your selected card with you for the entire day and study it in detail as often as possible. How you treat the card will depend on which card you have selected:

- **Major Arcana**: Allow that side of your character to surface for the day and notice your feelings and thoughts. Connect these with the symbols on the cards and get to know this side of you.
- **Minor Arcana – Court cards**: Search for this person in your environment. You may intend spending the day with a person that you recognise in the Court cards and then 'accidentally' select this card. Guard against this as it will limit you considerably. The intention is for you to start searching.
- **Minor Arcana – numbered cards**: Be aware for the entire day of when this situation arises. Take particular note of why this happens and how you deal with it.

Once you have spent the day with a card, move it to a different area while still displaying it. Greet these cards in the morning as if they were friends and say goodnight before going to bed. This will

establish a close connection between yourself and your cards and they will then serve you well.

After 78 days it may become clear that some of the cards still feel a little foreign. Put these aside and repeat the exercise until you feel comfortable with all 78 cards.

# A Tarot spread

There are many different Tarot spreads that one can use. However, a very simple spread using only seven cards will be studied. This is called the Pyramid Spread and although it is simple, it can be enhanced by treating it almost like an onion; peeling it layer by layer.

Diagram 5.3 shows the position of the cards. They are interpreted as follows:

Card 1: Past Influences – This card will indicate either a person, circumstances or an inner situation that played a part in the past.

Card 2: Present Situation – This card will show you whether a person, circumstances or an inner situation is active in the present situation.

Card 3: Hopes/Fears – A positive card will indicate hopes while a negative card will indicate fears. An upside down positive card will indicate a tendency to attract the negative aspects in a positive situation.

Card 4: Obstacles/Conflict – This card will indicate the obstacles that need to be overcome or the conflict that can be expected.

Card 5: Outside Influences – The environment, attitude towards others and theirs towards you will be indicated in this card.

Card 6: Best Course of Action – Here is a possible way in which the problem can be dealt with.

Card 7: Final Outcome –This card is the probable outcome of the current situation should the advice given in card 6 be followed.

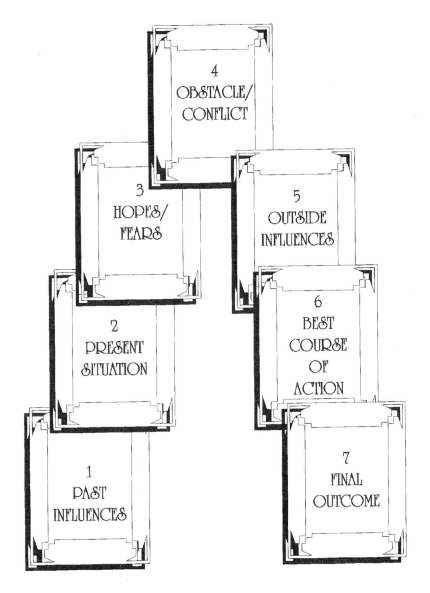

Diagram 5.3: The Tarot spread

# exercise 5
# a tarot reading

Before doing a Tarot spread, the following precautions need to be taken:

- Wash your hands and make sure that the surface upon which you intend working is clean and dust free.
- Ensure that all your cards are in the pack and in the upright position.
- Have a notebook and pen/pencil handy to make notes of the cards and how you interpret them.
- You may wish to light a candle or a stick of incense to create a peaceful atmosphere.

The Tarot spread is done by following the steps below without taking any short-cuts:

- Hold the cards in your left hand and lay your right hand over them. Visualise a bright light entering your crown chakra and allow this light to travel through your body, down your arms and out through your hands. This light will connect over the cards in your hands. Concentrate on your breathing while doing this.
- Now shift your awareness to the question in your mind. Really get in touch with all the feelings and thoughts that are connected to this question and while you do this, start shuffling the cards. Continue the shuffling for as long as you wish.
- If you are right-handed, only use your left hand to handle the cards from here on and if you are left-handed, only use your right hand. Cut the pack into three approximately equal packs towards you and reassemble the whole pack in the same direction (towards you) ensuring that the card that was originally at the top is now at the bottom.
- Without using your right/left hand, now place the cards in front of you, face down and upright. Lift the top card with your left hand and place it in position 1. (See Diagram 5.3.) Continue this until you have placed all seven cards in their correct positions.

- Now start interpreting the cards objectively. You may wish to make a note of which card is in which position in order to get some objective feedback from someone close to you.

- You may feel that you need to investigate this question a little more deeply. In this case continue placing the cards from position 1 to position 7 on top of the original spread. This new card will indicate the energies at a deeper level, almost, as I mentioned before, like peeling an onion.

- Once you have completed your spread, place the cards together in the upright positions and allow the light to enter them once again. Thank them for serving you and keep them in a very special place.

# 6 GEMATRIA AND NUMEROLOGY

*Gematria is the deeper meaning of Hebrew words. Hebrew is often referred to as the Holy language and Hebrew words such as 'Amen' and 'Hallelujah' are used all around the world. Hebrew words have inner meanings that manifest themselves into words very much as the aura manifests itself in the physical body.*

*The 22 letters of the Hebrew Aleph Beth are on the 22 paths of the Tree of Life and it is believed that these 22 letters were created long before the universe. The 22 letters of the Aleph Beth then presented themselves to the Father–Mother deity in reverse order, and asked to be the channel through which the universe and all its contents were to be created. The Mother–Father deity allowed each letter to channel only a portion of the light.*

# Examples of Gematria

There are some beautiful examples of Gematria in the Old Testament. One worth mentioning, referred to in Chapter 1, involves Abraham and his wife Sarah. Abraham's name was originally Abram (אברם) and Sarah's was Sarai (שרי). God told Abram that in order to see the future of the Israelites, he had to study the planets. Abram did this and soon discovered the influence that the planets have on man. He realised that there were no children in his future and he asked God about this.

God told Abram to add the *He* of his name (JOHOVAH – YHIH) to their names. The *He* in the name Johovah represents fertility. Abram

( אברם ) became Abraham ( אברהם ) and Sarai ( שרי ) became Sarah
( שרה ). They had their first child soon thereafter.

The word 'letter' in Hebrew is *ot* and also means 'signal'. Therefore,
when we see a Hebrew letter, we need to see the signal behind this
letter. Similarly, the word 'hand' in Hebrew is *yad* (spelled *yud daleth*)
and calculates to 14 (*yud* = 10 *daleth* = 4; 10 + 4 = 14) indicating that
there are 14 joints in the hand. Another example is the word *ozen*,
meaning 'ear'. By rearranging the Hebrew letters, the word *izoen*
(meaning 'balance') is found, indicating that physical balance lies
within the ear. Chapter 8 explores the power of the Aleph Beth further.

# The Aleph Beth

Table 6.1: The Aleph Beth and the 22 paths

| Path no. | Hebrew letter | | Num. value | Path no. | Hebrew letter | | Num. value | Path no. | Hebrew letter | | Num. value |
|---|---|---|---|---|---|---|---|---|---|---|---|
| 11 | Aleph | א | 1 | 20 | Yud | י | 10 | 29 | Qoph | ק | 100 |
| 12 | Beth | ב | 2 | 21 | Caph | כ | 20 | 30 | Resh | ר | 200 |
| 13 | Gimel | ג | 3 | 22 | Lamed | ל | 30 | 31 | Shin | ש | 300 |
| 14 | Daleth | ד | 4 | 23 | Mem | מ | 40 | 32 | Tav | ת | 400 |
| 15 | He | ה | 5 | 24 | Nun | נ | 50 | | | | |
| 16 | Vav | ו | 6 | 25 | Samesh | ס | 60 | | | | |
| 17 | Zain | ז | 7 | 26 | Ayin | ע | 70 | | | | |
| 18 | Cheth | ח | 8 | 27 | Pe | פ | 80 | | | | |
| 19 | Tet | ט | 9 | 28 | Tzaddi | צ | 90 | | | | |

The 22 letters in the Aleph Beth are grouped in Table 6.1 into three
categories. The first includes the letters Aleph to Tet, each with a
numerical value below 10. The second group includes the letters Yud
to Tzaddi, with numerical values in tens. The third group includes the
final four letters, Qoph to Tav, with numerical values in hundreds.

This divides the Aleph Beth into three spiritual levels, the first being
the lowest and the last (hundreds) the highest. Aleph ( א ) in the
first group represents the middle column on the Tree of Life, Mem
( מ ) in the second group the left column, and Shin ( ש ) the right.

# Numerology

Numerology, like Gematria, has an element of mystery attached to it. Yet both are practical calculations that anyone can use in everyday life.

The first step in teaching yourself numerology is to convert the alphabet into numbers. There are 26 letters in the alphabet, but we will work only with single-digit numbers. The number 26 will therefore become 8 (2+6=8), etc. In total the following applies:

| | | |
|---|---|---|
| 1 - A J S | 2 - B K T | 3 - C L U |
| 4 - D M V | 5 - E N W | 6 - F O X |
| 7 - G P Y | 8 - H Q Z | 9 - I R |

## Numerology and the Tree of Life

Every number has a potential. These potentials tie in with the ten spheres on the Tree of Life. They are as follows:

### 0   Negative Veils

The void between non-existence and existence. The symbolical representation of zero is the circle that a snake forms when it eats its own tail, i.e. living off itself like the universe that is a closed system.

### 1   Kether

The first step of existence. This number is represented symbolically by a single point that is not linked to any other. Any number can be divided and multiplied by the number 1 and the result will be the same as the original. On a personal level the number 1 indicates new beginnings, leadership, etc.

### 2   Chockmah

Duality of opposites. The number 2 is represented by a line that is formed when two points are connected. This number is about balance.

Like a coin that has two sides, one can only see one side at a time. The wisdom that is found in Chockmah is needed in order to be aware of the second side. In order for the Light-filled being (number 1) to share Her Love, it was necessary to create the opposite qualities (number 2).

## 3    Binah

Number 3 stands for creativity. Once the masculine and feminine parts of God became one (Numbers 1 and 2 and the First World) the entire universe was created. The understanding that we find in Binah was used in the process of the Creation. The number 3 is represented by a triangle that is formed when three points are connected. This triangle also represents that Spirit as a whole.

## 4    Chesed

Number 4 is represented by the pyramid and the square that is formed when four points are connected. The number 4 indicates practicality and order and Chesed is the level that can be used for greater abundance and organisation. When we apply the potential of number 4 to the qualities of Chesed, discipline in personal love, we will create peace and order in our lives.

## 5    Geburah

The number 5 is represented by the pentacle, which symbolises the five limbs of man. The number 5 indicates change and adaptability. Man is an ever-changing being and in order to use the qualities of Geburah (personal will) we need to be adaptable and ever-changing; breaking down the old to create space for the new.

## 6    Tiph-Ereth

The number 6 is represented by the six-pointed Star of David, which is a double triangle. The Spirit has the 'desire to share' and when man was created, he had to have the 'desire to receive' only to enable the Spirit to 'share'. The double triangle shows this relationship and Tiph-Ereth is the sphere on the centre of the Tree of Life, the

balancing point between the Spirit and the individual. On a personal level the number 6 indicates responsibility, commitment and family.

# 7 Netzach

The mysterious God-Force that rules nature is governed by the number 7. It is interesting to note that there are seven spheres below the Abyss. Seven (3+4=7) and twelve (3x4=12) are the two numbers that govern time in our universe; there are 7 days in a week and 12 months in a year and twice 12 hours in a day. Netzach is the level of feeling and is mysterious in itself. The symbol attached to the number 7 is the Seal of Solomon, which is the Star of David (number 6) with a point of spirit in the centre (number 1).

# 8 Hod

The number 8 is symbolised by the cube, the sign for eternity and the Kundalini. The figure 8 in itself symbolises two spheres; one indicating the spirit and the other the material world. The personal meaning of the number 8 is control, intellect and money matters. Hod is the level of thought, which in turn is a lower form of will.

# 9 Yesod

The number 9 is symbolised by the triple trinity (3x3=9). Pregnancy lasts for nine months and can be taken as creating and multiplying. The personal meaning of the number 9 is caring for humanity, emotions, creativity and letting go. Yesod is the level of the subconscious, where all the emotions are stored. It is believed that God descended onto earth nine times.

# 10 Malchuth

Malchuth is symbolised by two intercepting pentangles that illustrate man and his five limbs in an upright position and in an upside-down, evil position. This clearly shows that there are two sides to every person. The number 10 is a combination of the numbers 1 and 0, and the qualities of both these are visible when applied to our

senses. It is believed that the tenth time God descends to earth will be the final time during which the earth will be destroyed and a new one will be created from the rubble of the old.

# Practical numerology

There are various ways in which numerology can be applied to everyday life. The different numbers and the various letters associated with numbers 1–9 should now be clear.

In order to demonstrate numerology, we will take my name as an example. You may wish to do your name at the same time. Write the name down in large block letters.

K A T E   R H E E D E R S

Convert the letters of the name into numbers. For example K is the eleventh letter in the alphabet. It's number is 2 (11=1+1=2). E is the fifth, so its number is 5. Write the equivalent numbers of all the vowels above the name and all the consonants below the name as follows:

```
 1  5       5 5   5
 K A T E   R H E E D E R S
 2  2       9 8       4   9 1
```

The following information can now be gained using the above example:

## Soul number

The soul number is calculated by adding all the values of the vowels together: 1 + 5 + 5 + 5 + 5 = 21. The total is added up until you get a single-digit number: 2 + 1 = 3. This will be indicated as 21/3 from here on.

## Personality number

The personality number is calculated by adding all the consonants in the name: 2 + 2 + 9 + 8 + 4 + 9 + 1 = 35/8.

74

# NAME NUMBER

The name number is the total of all the numbers in the name. In other words, it is the total of the soul and the personality numbers: 3 + 8 = 11/2.

For the next set of numbers, make a table and count how many times certain numbers occur in the name. The table should look like this:

| | | | | | |
|---|---|---|---|---|---|
| 1——2 | | 4——1 | | 7——0 |
| 2——2 | | 5——4 | | 8——1 |
| 3——0 | | 6——0 | | 9——2 |

# KARMIC NUMBER

Notice which of the numbers are not represented in the name at all. In the example above it is numbers 3, 6 and 7. These are known as karmic numbers.

# INTENSITY NUMBER

The number that is repeated most often constitutes the intensity number. In the example above the number 5 is repeated four times and is therefore the intensity number of the author.

# DESTINY NUMBER

For the destiny number, study the date of birth. First convert the month to the equivalent number. January = 1, February = 2, etc. The date of birth we will use as an example is 22 June 1957.

    2 2 – 0 6 – 1 9 5 7

The date of birth, including the century (19) is added up in total: 2 + 2 + 6 + 1 + 9 + 5 + 7 = 32/5.

# PERSONAL YEAR NUMBER

The day and month of birth is used to calculate the personal year number. First establish whether the birthday of the person has

75

already taken place during the current year. If it has then add the day and month of birth to the present year (1995): 2 + 2 + 6 + 1 + 9 + 9 + 5 = 34/7. If the birthday has not taken place, add the day and month of birth to the previous year.

## Personal month number

This number is calculated by adding the personal year number to the number of the present month (November, 11): 7 + 11 = 18/9.

## Personal day number

This number is calculated by adding the personal month number to the current date: 9 + 9 = 18/9, assuming it is the 9th today.

# Application of information

The above calculations can now be summarised as follows:

| | |
|---|---|
| Soul number | 21/3 |
| Personality number | 35/8 |
| Name number | 11/2 |
| Karmic numbers | 3, 6, 7 |
| Intensity number | 5 |
| Destiny number | 32/5 |
| Personal year number | 34/7 |
| Personal month number | 18/9 |
| Personal day number | 18/9 |

In order to relate the above information, imagine life as a road that is travelled between birth and death. Refer to Diagram 6.1.

The road on which one has to travel is indicated by the destiny number. The soul number shows the capabilities of the engine in the vehicle in which this road is being travelled. The personality number indicates the appearance of the vehicle from the outside and the name number helps in understanding what type of driving skill is necessary in order to drive this vehicle. The karmic numbers show us certain defects on the vehicle, such as smooth tyres or

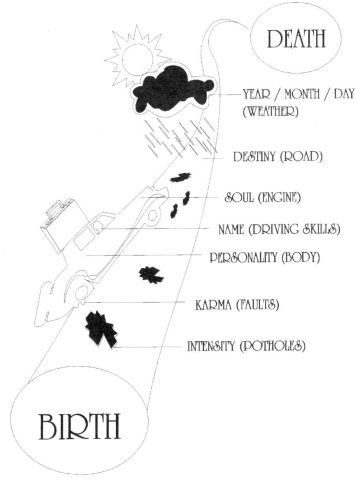

Diagram 6.1: Numerological road of life

maybe a faulty door handle, while the intensity number indicates the way in which the driver overcomes potholes in the road. The personal year, month and day numbers can be compared to seasonal changes that will occur on the road.

# EXERCISE 6
# GOAL SETTING

Numerology is a wonderful tool that can be used to achieve almost anything. But in order to make dreams come true, one first has to have dreams. Many people, have no idea what they want in life, let alone why they are here.

It is therefore important to establish what you want. Make sure that this dream is broken down into 'bite-size chunks' that can realistically be achieved within the period, and write these down. Calculate your potentials for the present year, month and day. Now try to relate your current situation to the example below.

Let us say that my goal is to have my own restaurant. This is obviously an expensive dream and in order to get there in the future, I need to start small.

**Year 1**. I find myself a small, affordable, mobile hot-dog stand and I move it to an area where I can immediately start trading. (New beginning)

**Year 2**. Competition moves in next door in the form of another hot-dog stand. My future does not look so bright now. (Balance/Competition)

**Year 3**. In order to continue working towards my dream, I start selling hamburgers as well, instead of closing down and moving to another spot. (Creativity)

**Year 4**. Since I am now selling both hot-dogs and hamburgers, I need to be practical. My organisation skills have effectively to be doubled. (Practicality)

**Year 5**. Having gone through the previous four steps and having learned more about the trade, I can now change my sauces and the name of my business. (Change)

**Year 6**. During this year I put my shoulder to the wheel and take responsibility for my business. Commitment is necessary to make a success of any venture. (Commitment)

**Year 7**. This is the year during which the business is on a roll and I can now assess my life and start planning for the future. (Spiritual/Prioritising)

**Year 8**. Having made the decision in the previous year, I can now sell my business. (Control and money matters)

**Year 9**. The business is handed over to the new owner during this year and plans are made for the next business venture. (Letting go)

**Year 10**. I can now use money from the sale of my hot-dog stand to buy myself a Chinese take-away that is a step closer to my final goal, i.e. my own restaurant. (New beginning)

Use your own example and slot it into this sequence. Decide where you want to go and start working out the steps that you need to take in order to get there.

# 7

# pLANETS ANÒ CRYSTALS

*Fashion a breastplate for making decisions – the work of a
skilled craftsman. Make it like the ephod; of gold, and of
blue, purple and scarlet yarn, and of finely twisted linen. It
is to be square – a span [approximately 22 cm] long and a
span wide – and folded double. Then mount four rows of
precious stones on it. In the first row there shall be a ruby,
a topaz and a beryl; in the second row a turquoise, a
sapphire and an emerald; in the third row a jacinth, an
agate and an amethyst; in the fourth row a chrysolite, an
onyx and a jasper. Mount them in gold filigree settings.
There are to be twelve stones, one for each of the names of
the sons of Israel, each engraved like a seal with the name
of one of the twelve tribes.*

Exodus 28: 15–21

*I*n ancient times crystals were referred to as ancient ice, mainly due to
their appearance. A third of the earth's crust consists of silicon oxide
which is especially common in sandy areas. During times when the
crust of the earth moves, the silicon oxide is shifted into the depths of
the earth, where it melts due to volcanic eruptions. When the melted
silicon oxide cools slowly, crystals are formed. The colour, structure
and density of the crystal is dependent on the other metals present in
its environment during crystallisation.

Crystals are widely used in modern technology. Probably the best
example of this is quartz watches. When an electrical current is
introduced into a silicon chip (none other than a crystal), a fixed
frequency of vibration results. This can be compared with electrons

*jumping off the surface of the crystal, which in turn moves the mechanics of the watch. Quartz watches are well known for their precision.*

# Where do crystals come from?

Crystals grow in cavities (Pregmatites) deep within the earth and these are often referred to as nature's jewel boxes. Crystals are mined very much like gold, diamonds and coal. Dynamite is often used to blast open the pregmatites in order to get to the crystals. Needless to say, this often causes tremendous damage to these beautiful structures that have taken many years to form.

Tumbled semi-precious stones have their origin in the same place although these crystals have spent long periods in a river bed where they have scraped against other similar stones, resulting in a polished appearance.

Some crystals will continue to grow new structures on the surfaces of the original crystal, even though they have been removed from their place of origin.

# Why are they important?

Crystals are important in the Age of Aquarius because they come from the earth in much the same way as man comes from God. The crystal is not the earth but is created by the earth.

Crystals have been found to date back as far as 3000 BC. When Moses received the Ten Commandments on Mount Sinai, God also gave him the design of the High Priest's breastplate. The breastplate contained 12 stones set in four horizontal and three vertical rows. When the High Priest wore the breastplate, the stones lost their

shine whenever he came into contact with a thief. It is also often debated whether the inscription of the Ten Commandments was made on sapphire or lapis lazuli.

Crystals are amplifiers, clarifiers, channellers and storage vessels. Crystals and mediums together have channelled all the present knowledge on the ancient civilisation of Atlantis. It is believed that Atlantis was situated in the Atlantic Ocean between the lower part of North America and North Africa. The legend of Atlantis is filled with descriptions of miracles and magic. Crystals are believed to have been used there to generate electricity and diagnose illnesses.

# how can we use them?

Crystals can be used with light and love or with ignorance. Owing to the fact that crystals are storage vessels, insights gained during meditation can be stored inside them. Clarification can be gained during meditation and the messages amplified. Thereby universal energies can be channelled through the crystal. Crystals can also be used to absorb negativity.

When crystals are used for their beauty only, they will have a harmonious influence in our lives. A crystal placed inside a room will start having an influence within 10 days. There will be more peace and harmony in this room.

# Crystals and planets

Before a crystal is formed, it is a seed deep in the crust of the earth. These seeds need moisture and heat to grow and this is supplied by the earth. The other planets in the solar system influence them during their growing process, producing all their unique qualities. The same principle applies to man, who is influenced by the various planets in the solar system every day.

# PLANETS AND THE TREE OF LIFE

Every sphere on the Tree of Life has a specific planet associated with it. It is interesting to note how much alike the solar system (Diagram 7.1) and the three-dimensional Tree of Life (Diagram 3.5) look. For readers familiar with astrology it will be easier to make the connections. Should you be unfamiliar with this topic, try to make the connection through the crystals.

The solar system is divided into an inner and an outer solar system by the asteroid belt that lies between Mars (Geburah) and Jupiter (Chesed), with Mars in the inner and Jupiter in the outer solar system. The Veil separates the Tree at the level of Tiph-Ereth and I sometimes wonder if this veil is not perhaps the equivalent of the asteroid belt.

Another 'coincidence' is the fact that the planet Uranus, which orbits between Saturn (Binah) and Neptune (Chockmah) is not associated with any spheres on the Tree of Life. Jupiter, Saturn and Neptune all radiate more heat back into space than they absorb from the Sun. Uranus almost has no excess heat to radiate back. The Abyss lies between Binah/Chockmah and Geburah/Chesed. Maybe the planet Uranus is the equivalent of the Abyss.

# CRYSTALS AND THE TREE OF LIFE

Every sphere and path has a crystal or a precious stone associated with it. These stones/crystals carry the same peculiar qualities that are in the sphere and in the associated planet. The associated planet had a major influence on the stone during its formation and continues having a connection on the awareness on that specific level.

Table 7.1 shows the 10 spheres, their planetary correspondences and the crystals associated with both these:

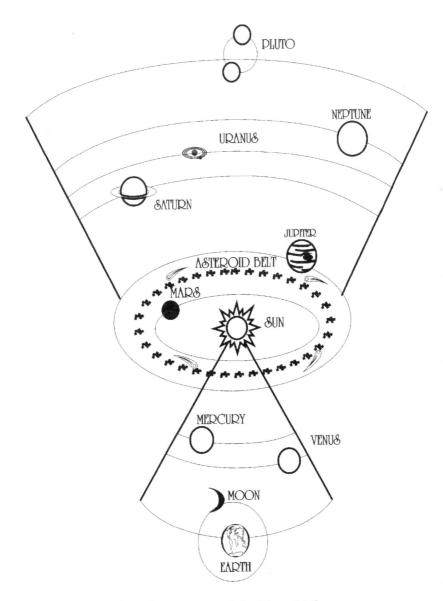

Diagram 7.1: The solar system and the Tree of Life

Table 7.1: Spheres and associated cystals

| No. | Sphere | Traditional | Planet | Planetary association |
|---|---|---|---|---|
| 1 | Kether | Diamond | Pluto | Agate, ruby, topaz |
| 2 | Chockmah | Star ruby | Neptune | Jade, tourmaline, turquoise |
| 3 | Binah | Star sapphire | Saturn | Jet, black and white onyx |
| 4 | Chesed | Amethyst | Jupiter | Amethyst, malachite |
| 5 | Geburah | Ruby | Mars | Carnelian, bloodstone |
| 6 | Tiph-Ereth | Topaz | Sun | Emerald, red onyx, ruby |
| 7 | Netzach | Emerald | Venus | Lapis lazuli, tourmaline |
| 8 | Hod | Opal | Mercury | Hematite, sapphire |
| 9 | Yesod | Quartz crystal | Moon | Moonstone, pearl |
| 10 | Malchuth | Rock crystal | Earth | Tiger's eye |

Looking at these stones in more detail from Malchuth up to Kether it is interesting to note how the stones themselves reflect the qualities of the various spheres.

## Malchuth

The planet associated with Malchuth is Earth. Earth is the only planet in the solar system known to support life. The continental and oceanic plates are slowly drifting, bringing constant change. Earth is 149.6m km away from the Sun and has only one moon. Symbolically Earth represents stability and the function of the five senses.

The stone associated with the planet Earth is the tiger's eye, a very rich, earthy stone that is believed to sharpen the conscious mind. In Africa this stone symbolises death because it resembles the eyes of a crocodile.

The stone traditionally associated with Malchuth is rock crystal, used for building blocks in ancient China and as talismans by the Cherokee Indians. It was believed that it brought its owner great power in hunting and divining. Rock crystal is the most freely available crystal on earth.

## Yesod

Yesod is associated with the Moon. The Moon's orbit is around Earth and it is forever changing between full moon and dark moon

through its waxing and waning cycle. This ever-changeable cycle is within each individual. Yesod is enclosed by the other elements of the personality (feelings, thoughts and senses) and the subtle changes taking place are not always recognised. During a solar eclipse the Moon moves between the Sun (Tiph-Ereth) and the Earth (Malchuth). This happens in our lives when we loose sight of the real 'I'.

The stones associated with the Moon are the moonstone and the pearl. The moonstone has a pearly-white surface that changes as the light varies. It helps us deal with emotional difficulties and in finding the balance between giving and receiving love. The pearl is a very feminine stone that restores harmony in an irritable situation. It turns a negative situation into a positive, loving environment.

The traditional stone associated with Yesod is the quartz crystal. There are many types of quartz, such as clear, smoky and rose. Clear quartz is particularly helpful in dealing with past experiences and in overcoming stagnation; smoky quartz absorbs negativity; and rose quartz soothes us and helps us to overcome our fears.

# Hod

The planet associated with Hod is Mercury. Mercury is heavily cratered and almost airless and is considered a dead planet. It has a very thin atmosphere consisting of sodium and helium. In astrology and myth, Mercury represents the 'trickster' figure on the borders of the conscious and unconscious minds. Our thoughts (Hod) are often also 'tricksters' that bring about uncertainty and insecurity without any reason.

The stones associated with Mercury are hematite and sapphire. Hematite is known as a red oxide of iron and was believed to be particularly powerful, granting invulnerability when legal battles were being fought. It is sometimes associated with Mars (Geburah), the God of War. Geburah lies above Hod on the left column of the Tree of Life. This is, in a sense, higher form of thought.

The sapphire is in the High Priest's breastplate in the middle of the second row of stones. Belief has it that the Ten Commandments were engraved on slabs of sapphire, although there is some doubt because of the assumed size of the tablets. Sapphire brings truth

and wisdom into our lives. In ancient times it was used for infections and to counteract poisoning.

The traditional stone associated with Hod is the opal. This stone is sensitive and should be kept separate from others.  It loves water and should be soaked in cold water often. It was believed to help women in childbirth to let go and relax. This stone can increase psychic awareness by helping us to let go of thoughts and listen to the inner voice.

## Netzach

The planet associated with Netzach is Venus.  Venus is almost the same size as Earth and has a very dense atmosphere, creating a greenhouse effect. It is believed that there are many large, active volcanoes on its surface. In Greek mythology, the Goddess of Love is known as Venus. Feelings (Netzach) are a lower form of Love (Chesed).

The stones associated with Venus are lapis lazuli and tourmaline. The belief that the Ten Commandments were engraved on slabs of lapis lazuli is by far the stronger one due to the sizes available. It is known as the stone of the gods and it is said to guard against depression by counteracting darkness. This stone has the ability to keep us physically strong while waking up to the spirit.

Tourmaline is a relatively new stone (known since the eighteenth century) that provides balance between two opposing forces such as positive/negative, inner/outer, good/evil and life/death. It is therefore a very good protector that also helps us to forgive others.

The traditional stone associated with Netzach is the emerald. An emerald was in the breastplate in the first position on the second row, next to the sapphire. This stone is known as the Jewel of Venus, and it promotes fertility and love. The blue sapphire was used to aid chastity by protecting its wearer from unwanted intruders.

## Tiph-Ereth

The planet associated with Tiph-Ereth is the Sun. The Sun is the centre of our solar system and it is the gravitational attraction of

this planet that controls the orbits of the other planets. The Sun consists mainly of hydrogen and helium, sending out energy as it slowly rotates on its own axis. Tiph-Ereth is the centre of the Tree of Life and the balancing point between our spiritual and physical selves.

The stones associated with the Sun are the emerald, onyx and ruby. See Netzach for information on the emerald. An onyx was placed in the middle position on the fourth row of the breastplate. Onyx is found in various colours and, in general, balances the feminine and masculine sides. The red onyx brings this balance strongly into our physical beings.

The ruby brings the 'desire to share' to the surface and at the same time helps us deal with the resentment we may build up if we feel we are sharing without receiving. This is a stone that lies close to the soul. The lighter rubies are considered to be female stones.

The traditional stone associated with Tiph-Ereth is the topaz. This stone was placed in the second position in the first row of stones on the breastplate. It relieves stress during sleep and adds new energy to life. In ancient times, topaz was used to cure loss of sight and to prevent colds.

## Geburah

The planet associated with Geburah is Mars, which is the outer planet in the inner solar system. Two moons orbit Mars. The surface of Mars consists mainly of iron-rich dunes and channels, possibly formed by water in the past. It is often referred to as the 'red planet' due to its red dust blown around by strong winds. This may be one of the reasons why myth refers to the God of War as Mars.

The traditional stone associated with Geburah is the ruby (see Tiph-Ereth) and the stones associated with Mars are the carnelian and bloodstone. The carnelian is known as the motivator which helps bring ideas to the fore. It gives the courage to pursue dreams and aids in expressing needs. During the seventeenth century it was believed that this stone protected its wearer from falling roofs and walls.

In ancient times it was believed that the wearer of a bloodstone would receive all that was asked for. In more modern times, the bloodstone is used to help women ease their menstrual cycle. It is a calming stone that improves the circulation.

## Chesed

The planet associated with Chesed is Jupiter, situated in the first position in the outer solar system. There are 16 moons orbiting Jupiter. Jupiter is known as the largest planet in the solar system and measures approximately one-tenth of the Sun. Jupiter is often described as a whirling ball of gas that is compressed to liquid in the centre.

The stone associated with Jupiter is malachite. This stone was and still is appropriate for children. The ancients believed that when a small piece was attached to the crib, evil spirits were kept at bay and the child slept peacefully through the night. Today it is used to promote healthy teeth in children and it calms and soothes a child during teething.

The stone traditionally associated with Chesed is the amethyst. The most common use of this stone during Roman times was to prevent drunkenness by placing it in a glass of wine. Its power to save the wearer from drunkenness is still a popular application. Amethyst is known to be a strong transmitter that lifts the spirit to greater heights.

## Binah

The planet associated with Binah is Saturn. The majestic ring that circles Saturn consists of countless icy particles. There are 17 moons orbiting Saturn. Saturn is known as the second largest planet in the solar system and has a hydrogen-rich atmosphere.

The stones associated with Saturn are onyx and jet. Onyx is discussed under Tiph-Ereth. In ancient times, jet ornaments were worn directly on the skin and it was believed that it became part of the soul. It is also believed to protect its wearer against others undermining authority and against jealousy. It is considered to be a stone for the cynics.

The stone traditionally associated with Binah is the star sapphire. For more details on the sapphire see under Hod. The star sapphire is a variety of sapphire that, when polished into a dome shape, reflects light into three crossed lines that produce a star. This stone is often referred to as the destiny stone, because it helps us to reach for the stars.

## Chockmah

The planet associated with Chockmah is Neptune. Neptune has an atmosphere containing methane and its surface is disturbed by great storms. There are eight moons orbiting Neptune, of which the largest is Triton.

The stones associated with Neptune are jade, tourmaline and turquoise. A great variety of colours are available in jade and the colour itself will add extra dimension to the various stones. In general jade is a good friendship stone that heals and balances. It absorbs the fears that prevent us from expressing love. This is a good stone for bone growth and blood purification.

For details on tourmaline, see under Netzach. In ancient times turquoise was used particularly to protect horses and their riders against injury. In modern times, it is believed that it helps its wearer to find the courage to address large groups of people. Turquoise has a large copper content and this may be the reason why it is so effective with rheumatism and arthritis.

The stone traditionally associated with Chockmah is the star ruby. For details on ruby, see under Tiph-Ereth. The star and dark rubies, although having the same qualities as the lighter ones, are considered to be male stones. These bring the 'desire to share', which in itself can be considered a feminine quality, strongly to the masculine side.

## Kether

The planet associated with Kether is Pluto, which is the outermost, coldest and smallest planet in the solar system. It is believed to be a snowball of methane and water mixed with rock and, together with its only moon, it is often referred to as a double planet.

The stones associated with Pluto are the agate, ruby and topaz. In 1709 literature was discovered in Vienna telling the story of a Brazilian priest who invented an airship. Over its navigator was a network filled with coral-agates that the sun magnetised, thereby drawing the ship into the air. In modern times agate is believed to protect its wearer from dangers and physical injury. It has an inner–outer balancing effect in that it secures the physical and emotional aspects of its wearer. The ruby and the topaz are discussed under Tiph-Ereth.

The stone traditionally associated with Kether is the diamond. It is very true that 'Diamonds are a girl's best friend'. Diamonds are often referred to as the jewel of the future, while quartz is the gem of today. In ancient times it was believed that diamonds provided protection against the plague. It is interesting to note that once the plague attacked, it was the poorer people, who could not afford diamonds, that suffered most.

# EXERCISE 7
# CRYSTAL MEDITATION

1. Sit or lie in a comfortable position and close your eyes. Allow your breathing to fall into a rhythm without any force. Be aware of your thoughts, feelings and body without hanging on to any of them. Just allow them to come and then let them go.
2. Now imagine yourself walking towards your inner sanctuary – that place where you feel completely safe and secure; the most beautiful place in the world for you. Feel the grass under your feet; smell the flowers around you; hear the wind blowing through the trees; feel the sun shine on your face. Spend some time in your inner sanctuary and explore a little.
3. When you are ready, look around until you find a bench under a tree. This bench may be any shape, any colour and made from any material you wish. Walk towards the bench, sit or lie down and make yourself comfortable. Allow all the elements of nature around you to continue at their own pace and rhythm and become part of them. Just simply be.

4. Notice a flash across your closed eyelids. Something has reflected the sunlight onto you. Now imagine that you get up from the bench and walk towards where you think the flash came from. Spend some time looking at the ground and search for an object that can reflect the sunlight.

5. Imagine you find the most beautiful crystal that you have ever seen. Allow this crystal to have all the characteristics that you wish it to have. Study the crystal in detail by feeling it, tasting it and smelling it. Place the crystal on your cheek and feel the icy surface that gave it its name of ancient ice. Realise that this particular crystal had been waiting for you for many years and the time is finally here.

6. Now imagine yourself moving into the crystal. Feel the icy texture around your whole body and enjoy the refreshing feeling that you experience. Explore the cavities, clouds and rainbows inside this beautiful crystal. You will find that somewhere inside the crystal is an altar. Move towards this altar and you will find a closed book on top. This book has your name engraved in gold on the front cover.

7. Before you open this book, ensure that you have a question to ask. Clarify your question to yourself and only once you are sure of what it is that you need to know, open the book at random. Now read the page where you have opened the book. Do not abuse this gift by going further, instead accept this gift with gratitude.

8. When you have finished, thank the book for its wisdom, close it and move towards the edge of the crystal. Find your way out of the crystal and when you are ready, place the crystal where you first found it. You can visit the crystal again in the future.

9. Bring your awareness back to the surface on which you sit. When you are ready, open your eyes, feeling refreshed, enriched and wiser. Make a commitment to yourself about the information that you have gained during this exercise.

# 8 THE NEXT STEP

*The Qabalah can serve you well for the rest of this life if you choose to keep it alive. It is very easy to allow the Qabalah to become just another set of rules or simply another belief system.*

# A QABALISTIC DIARY

I would like to suggest you start a Qabalistic diary in which you record your insights. The Qabalah has traditional values, some of which I have covered in this book, and individual values that are uniquely your own. These individual values are the most important ones for you. Start recording them, thereby recognising your own evolution.

I see these individual values as a personal set of rules which I often refer to as my 'instruction manual'. We all have our own 'instruction manuals' that will determine our own rules. These are the 'measuring sticks' by which we judge ourselves, now and hereafter.

As an example, I would like to relate an incident in my life. My son had a white budgie and I made sure that good care was taken of it. I kept the budgie seed and the aniseed in identical containers and accidentally fed the budgie the aniseed. To cut a long story short, the budgie died and left me with incredible guilt feelings. These guilt feelings were obviously in my 'instruction manual'.

I was given an opportunity to correct the situation by rescuing another budgie that came walking down the road one day. This bird,

a yellow one, had its wings clipped and was unable to fly, or to fend for itself. I now make sure that the same situation does not repeat itself.

The age-old saying, 'Beauty is in the eye of the beholder,' means that in order to see beauty in others, you need to have that very same beauty within you first, or else you would not have the image by which to recognise it. People around us are our mirrors that reflect back to us an image of ourselves, positive and negative. Recognise why certain individuals irritate or upset you. These are indicators that will enable you to start looking within and finding those very qualities which, when put together, form your own personal 'instruction manual'.

# fURThER STUDY

I would like to stress, in my conclusion, that this book is only a brief introduction to the Qabalah. My personal interpretation played a big role and you may not necessarily agree with me on all points.

Should you wish to study the Qabalah in greater depth, I would like to suggest you find the nearest 'Kabbalah Learning Centre' – international branch addresses are given below. This is an international organisation headed by Rabbi Berg, who has written numerous in-depth studies on the Qabalah.

Should you wish to correspond with me, I will do my best to answer your letter personally. My postal address is:

Kate Rheeders
PO Box 15239
FARRARMERE
1518 Benoni
South Africa

# Kabbalah Learning Centres

**Main office**      83–4 115th Street
                     Richmond Hill
                     New York
                     USA
                     Tel: (718) 805-9122  Fax: (718) 805-5899

**United Kingdom**   PO Box 116
                     37 Store Street
                     London
                     Tel: 0181-914-7991

**United States**    39 South East lst Avenue
                     Boca Raton
                     Florida
                     Tel: (407) 347-7095  Fax: (407) 361-3132

                     1062 S. Robertson Boulevard
                     Los Angeles
                     California
                     Tel: (310) 657-5404  Fax: (310) 657-7774

**Canada**           678 Sheppard Avenue
                     W. Toronto
                     Ontario
                     Tel: (416) 631-9395  Fax: (416) 631-7841

**France**           20 Passage Turquetil
                     Paris
                     Tel: (331) 4356-0138  Fax: (331) 4356-2689

**Israel**           25 Bograshov Street
                     Tel Aviv
                     Tel: (972) 3-528-0570  Fax: (972) 3-201-258

**Mexico**           Ave. De Las Fuentas 218
                     Tecamachalco
                     Tel/Fax: (525) 589-4464

# OTHER TITLES IN THIS SERIES

**Astral Projection**   Is it possible for the soul to leave the body at will? In this book the traditional techniques used to achieve astral projection are described in a simple, practical way, and Out of the Body and Near Death Experiences are also explored.

**Astrology**   An exploration of how astrology helps us to understand ourselves and other people. Learn how to draw up and interpret a horoscope.

**Astrology and Health**   This book explains simply the symbolic richness of the zodiac signs and how they can illuminate our experience of health.

**Becoming Prosperous**   A guide to how *anyone* can feel and become more prosperous by focusing on state of mind and conscious thought. Practical exercises help readers develop personal strategies to become more prosperous, both financially and emotionally.

**Chakras**   The body's energy centres, the chakras, can act as gateways to healing and increased self-knowledge. This book shows you how to work with chakras in safety and with confidence.

**Channelling**   Channelling is the process by which ancient knowledge and wisdom are tapped and reclaimed for the enlightenment and enrichment of life in the present. This book offers simple techniques to become channels of awareness.

**Chinese Horoscopes**   In the Chinese system of horoscopes, the year of birth is all-important. *Chinese Horoscopes for beginners* tells you how to determine your own Chinese horoscope, what personality traits you are likely to have, and how your fortunes may fluctuate in years to come.

**Dowsing**   People all over the world have used dowsing since the earliest times. This book shows how to start dowsing – what to use, what to dowse, and what to expect when subtle energies are detected.

**Dream Interpretation**   This fascinating introduction to the art and science of dream interpretation explains how to unravel the meaning behind dream images to interpret your own and other people's dreams.

**Earth Mysteries**   What can we learn from observing the earth and the remains of our prehistoric ancestors? Explore ley lines, earth energies, astro-archaeology and sacred landscapes to expand your consciousness and achieve a better perspective on existence.

**Enlightenment**   Learn how you can experience primary enlightenment through tried-and-tested exercises which offer the tools to help you to find your own unique truth.

**Feng Shui**   This beginner's guide to the ancient art of luck management will show you how to increase your good fortune and well-being by harmonising your environment with the natural energies of the earth.

**Freeing Your Intuition**   Develop awareness of your intuition and make your own good fortune, increase your creative output and learn to recognise what you *know*, not just what you think.

**Gems and Crystals**   For centuries gems and crystals have been used as an aid to healing and meditation. This guide tells you all you need to know about choosing, keeping and using stones to increase your personal awareness and improve your well-being.

**Ghosts**   In this exploration of the shadowy world of ghosts, the author looks at poltergeists, hauntings, ghouls, phantoms of the living, the ouija board, ghost hunting, scientific proof of survival after death and the true meaning of Hallowe'en.

**The Goddess**   This book traces the development, demise and rebirth of the Goddess, looking at the worship of Her and retelling myths from all over the world.

**Graphology**   Graphology, the science of interpreting handwriting to reveal personality, is now widely accepted and used throughout the world. This introduction will enable you to make a comprehensive analysis of your own and other people's handwriting to reveal the hidden self.

**The Healing Powers of Plants**   Plants and herbs can be used to enhance everyday life through aromatheraphy, herbalism, homoeopathy and colour therapy. Their power can be used in cosmetics, meditation and home decoration.

**Herbs for Magic and Ritual**   This book looks at the well-known herbs and the stories attached to them. There is information on the use of herbs in essential oils and incense, and on their healing and magical qualities.

**I Ching**   The roots of *I Ching* or the *Book of Changes* lie in the time of the feudal mandarin lords of China, but its traditional wisdom is still relevant today. Using the original poetry in its translated form, this introduction traces its history, survival and modern-day applications.

**Interpreting Signs and Symbols**   The history of signs and symbols is traced in this book from their roots to the modern age. It also examines the way psychiatry uses symbolism, and the significance of doodles.

**The Language of Flowers**   Flowers can and do heal us, both emotionally and physically, with their smell and their beauty. By looking at these areas, together with superstitions associated with flowers and their links with New Age subjects, the author gives advice on how to enhance your life with flowers.

**Love Signs**   This is a practical introduction to the astrology of romantic relationships. It explains the different roles played by each of the planets, focusing particularly on the position of the Moon at the time of birth.

**The Magic and Mystery of Trees**   This book explores the many meanings of trees, from myth and folklore through ritual and seasonal uses to their 'spiritual essence' and esoteric meanings.

**Meditation**   This beginner's guide gives simple, clear instructions to enable you to start meditating and benefiting from this ancient mental discipline immediately. The text is illustrated throughout by full-colour photographs and line drawings.

**Mediumship**   Whether you want to become a medium yourself, or simply understand what mediumship is about, this book will give you the grounding to undertake a journey of discovery into the spirit realms.

**The Moon and You**   The phase of the Moon when you were born radically affects your personality. This book looks at nine lunar types – how they live, love, work and play, and provides simple tables to find out the phase of your birth.

**The Norse Tradition**   This book gives a comprehensive introduction to the Norse Tradition, a vibrant, living current within the multitude of spiritual paths of Paganism.

**Numerology**   Despite being scientifically based, numerology requires no great mathematical talents to understand. This introduction gives you all the information you will need to understand the significance of numbers in your everyday life.

**Numerology and Relationships**   This guide takes you step by step through the hidden meanings behind the important numbers in your life to discover more about you, your compatibilities with others and the crucial relationships with your parents, partner and children.

**Pagan Gods**   Looking at ancient gods and old stories, this guide explores the social and psychological issues affecting the role of men today. In these pages men of all ages and persuasions can find inspiration.

**Paganism**   Pagans are true Nature worshippers who celebrate the cycles of life. This guide describes pagan festivals and rituals and takes a detailed look at the many forms of paganism practised today.

**Palmistry**   Palmistry is the oldest form of character reading still in use. This illustrated guide shows you exactly what to look for and how to interpret what you find.

**Qabalah**   The Qabalah is an ancient Jewish system of spiritual knowledge centred on the Tree of Life. This guide explains how it can be used in meditation and visualisation, and links it to the chakras, yoga, colour therapy, crystals, Tarot and numerology.

**Reiki**   In this book you will find advice on how to learn Reiki, its application and potential, and you will be shown an avenue of understanding of this simple, practical technique which offers pain relief through meditation and laying-on of hands.

**Reincarnation and You**   What happens to us after death? Here, you will find practical advice on using dreams, recurrent visions, déjà vu and precognition to access hidden parts of your consciousness which recall or anticipate past and future lives.

**Runes**   The power of the runes in healing and giving advice about relationships and life in general has been acknowledged since the time of the Vikings. This book shows how runes can be used in our technological age to increase personal awareness and stimulate individual growth.

**Shamanism**   Shamanic technique offers direct contact with Spirit, vivid self-knowledge and true kinship with plants, animals and the planet Earth. This book describes the shamanic way, the wisdom of the Medicine Wheel and power animals.

**Some Traditional African Beliefs**   Fortune telling and healing are two of the aspects of traditional African spiritual life looked at in this book. Exercises based on ancient beliefs show you how to use the environment to find ways to harmonise modern urban life in a practical way.

**Spiritual Healing**   All healing starts with self, and the Universal Power which makes this possible is available to everyone. In this book there are exercises, techniques and guidelines to follow which will enable you to heal yourself and others spiritually.

**Star Signs**   This detailed analysis looks at each of the star signs in turn and reveals how your star sign affects everything about you. This book shows you how to use this knowledge in your relationships and in everyday life.

**Tantric Sexuality**   Tantric Buddhists use sex as a pleasurable path to enlightenment. This guide offers a radically different and exciting new dimension to sex, explaining practical techniques in a clear and simple way.

**Tarot**   Tarot cards have been used for many centuries. This guide gives advice on which sort to buy, where to get them and how to use them. The emphasis is on using the cards positively, as a tool for gaining self-knowledge, while exploring present and future possibilities.

**Visualisation**   This introduction to visualisation, a form of self-hypnosis widely used by Buddhists, will show you how to practise the basic techniques – to relieve stress, improve your health and increase your sense of personal well-being.

**Witchcraft**   This guide to the ancient religion based on Nature worship answers many of the questions and uncovers the myths and misconceptions surrounding witchcraft. Mystical rituals and magic are explained and there is advice for the beginner on how to celebrate the Sabbats.

**Working With Colour**   Colour is the medicine of the future. This book explores the energy of each colour and its significance, gives advice on how colour can enhance our well-being, and gives ideas on using colour in the home and garden.

**Your Psychic Powers**   Are you psychic? This book will help you find out by encouraging you to look more deeply within yourself. Psychic phenomena such as precognitive dreams, out of body travels and visits from the dead are also discussed in this ideal stepping stone towards a more aware you.

# To order this series

All books in this series are available from bookshops or, in case of difficulty, can be ordered direct from the publisher. Prices and availability subject to change without notice. Send your order with your name and address to: Hodder & Stoughton, Cash Sales Department, Bookpoint, 39 Milton Park, Abingdon, OXON, OX14 4TD, UK. If you have a credit card you may order by telephone – 01235 831700.

For sales in the following countries please contact:
UNITED STATES: Trafalgar Square (Vermont), Tel: 800 423 4525 (toll-free)
CANADA: General Publishing (Ontario), Tel: 445 3333
AUSTRALIA: Hodder & Stoughton (Sydney), Tel: 02 638 5299

## A BEGINNER'S GUIDE

# TAROT

### Kristyna Arcarti

You are about to take a financial risk and draw the Ace of pentacles. What does this suggest? Does the Lover card indicate a romance?

*Tarot – a beginner's guide* gives you the information you need to learn about yourself, and others, through the cards. Advice is given on what sort of cards you should buy and how you should use them. Fully illustrated in colour, each chapter explores a different aspect of the cards, explaining the meanings and interpretations. Practice sections put your knowledge to the test. The final chapter gives a sample reading and looks at the most popular spreads in use.

*'Here is a beautifully illustrated, nicely presented, excellent introduction on the Tarot. Beginners will learn much from this work.'* Prediction

## A BEGINNER'S GUIDE

# meditation

## Naomi Ozaniec

editation is a mental discipline which has been practised through the ages by people of many different cultures. It is a simple technique to learn which, when mastered, will help you to understand yourself better, relax mentally and think more clearly. *Meditation – a beginner's guide* explains the basic concepts and principles of meditation, gives clear instructions to enable you to start meditating immediately and provides practical advice on how to incorporate meditation into your life. Every chapter has a special section offering guidance on overcoming common problems and anxieties.

Naomi Ozaniec has studied meditation for over ten years. As a writer and teacher, she is experienced in helping beginners to get the most out of their practice.